Historical Documents
Advocating
Christian Union

in the hope of immortality

A. Campbell

Historical Documents

Advocating

Christian Union

Epoch-Making Statements by Leaders among
the Disciples of Christ for the Restora-
tion of the Christianity of the New
Testament—its Doctrines, its
Ordinances, and its
Fruits

Historical Introductions by
Charles Alexander Young
Managing Editor of THE CHRISTIAN CENTURY

College Press Publishing Co., Inc.
Joplin, Missouri

Reprinted and Distributed by
College Press Publishing Co., Inc.
P.O. Box 1132
Joplin, Mo. 64802
Don DeWelt, Editor
1985

International Standard
Book Number
0-89900-276-5

Contents

General Introduction

THE advocacy of Christian Union has become very popular in recent years. A hundred years ago the advocacy of Christian Union upon the New Testament basis was very unpopular. The Restoration movement of the Nineteenth Century placed large emphasis upon Christian Union as essentail to the conversion of the world. The prayer of our divine Lord, "that they all may be one, as thou, Father, art in me and I in thee, that they also may be one in us, that the world may believe that thou hast sent me "— became the favorite Scripture text of the Disciples of Christ. Four preachers — all originally Presbyterians — gave direction to this mighty movement for Christian Union. All four were deeply devout and highly educated men. The intellectual strength and princely personality of these four men still exert a commanding influence upon the Disciples of Christ. To preserve and extend this salutary influence in the interest of Christian Union and world wide evangelization is one purpose of the publication of the " Historical Documents " advocating Christian Union. These four spiritual

5

giants were Barton W. Stone, Thomas Campbell, Alexander Campbell, and Walter Scott. Originally we had planned to have in this volume extracts from Walter Scott representing views he held in common with his coadjutors on the personality and work of the Holy Spirit and the Messiahship. His two favorite themes were The Messiahship and the Holy Spirit. After he became a Baptist preacher he was the first man in modern times to present the elements of the gospel in their scriptural order. He urged persons who accepted the testimony of the Holy Spirit in regard to the divine personality of our Lord to publicly confess that "Jesus is the Christ, the Son of God," and he baptized "into the name of the Father and the Son and the Holy Spirit," that they might receive the remission of sins through the atoning blood of our divine Lord. The following is the plain but scriptural order in which Walter Scott presented the elements of the gospel:

"His first step was to fix upon the divinity of Christ as the central and controlling thought of the New Testament, and which he afterwards demonstrated and illustrated with a strength and felicity that has never been surpassed. Next, he arranged the elements of the

6

gospel in the simple and natural order of Faith,
Repentance, Baptism, Remission of Sins, and
Gift of the Holy Spirit; then made Baptism
the practical acceptance of the gospel on the
part of the penitent believer, as well as the
pledge or assurance of pardon on the part of
its author." (Life of Walter Scott, William
Baxter.)

In presenting the elements of the gospel his
advocacy made many things plain. "1. It introduced Faith on Evidence. 2. Repentance on
Motive. 3. Obedience on Authority. 4. It
put the gift of the Holy Spirit where the Scriptures put it. 5. It restored the creed of our
religion to its proper place and eminence above
all other things in the gospel. 6. It limited the
faith and love of the gospel to a person; not a
doctrine or a fact. 7. It delivered from false
centers of affection, as well as false centers of
faith; for while it held up the Lord Jesus in
his divine nature for faith, it also held him up
in his offices for affection; for it baptized men
for remission of sins by his blood. A doctrine
was no longer the center."

Neither Mr. Campbell, Mr. Scott, nor any
of the " Reformers " ever taught that baptism
had any saving quality in itself. We are not

saved by any or all the conditions of pardon independently of the grace of God, the blood of Christ, and the Holy Spirit. Baptism is the divinely appointed act by which the penitent believer appropriates the blood of Christ for the remission of sins.

However, when we found this book had grown to nearly four hundred pages without the extracts from Walter Scott's " Messiah-ship," we reluctantly omitted them. Barton W. Stone was principally responsible for the " Last Will and Testament of the Springfield Presbytery." While Mr. Gates in his recent book, the " Early Relation and Separation of the Baptists and Disciples," dates the formal beginning of the Disciples of Christ as a separate religious body pleading for Christian Union about 1830, B. B. Tyler in his History of the Disciples of Christ goes back to the " Last Will and Testament of the Springfield Presbytery " in 1804. We consider this literary monument in the advocacy of Christian Union worthy a place among the " Historical Documents."

The " Declaration and Address " of Thomas Campbell is really the Magna Charta of the Restoration Movement of the Nineteenth Century. It is the greatest document ever written

in the advocacy of Christian Union. The
Analysis by Errett Gates, Ph.D., appeared first
as a series of articles in the Christian Century.
While Christian Union never had a greater
protagonist than Alexander Campbell, it is
evident to every intelligent reader of the Declaration and Address that Thomas Campbell
laid the foundation for the greatest religious
movement of the Nineteenth Century — a
movement which primarily advocated Christian
Union as essential to the conversion of the
world, but may ultimately advocate the conversion of the world through the preaching of
the Gospel of Christ as the essential of restoring Christian Union. "The Sermon on the
Law," by Alexander Campbell, "Our Position," by Isaac Errett ,and "The World's
Need of Our Plea," by J. H. Garrison, were
given a place among the "Historical Documents" advocating Christian Union, for two
reasons. They are all three worthy of preservation in permanent form, and they represent
the literary work of the three foremost editors
among the Disciples of Christ who have given
their lives to the advocacy of Christian Union.
Our original purpose two years ago was to
republish the "Declaration and Address" of

Thomas Campbell, with the Analysis so carefully prepared by Mr. Gates. The plan of presenting to the religious world the literary history of the Disciples of Christ for the first one hundred years from the date of the " Last Will and Testament of the Springfield Presbytery," grew out of this original purpose. We hope the readers of these " Historical Documents " advocating Christian Union, may not only experience some of the joy we have felt in editing them, but may also be influenced to encourage every sincere effort from every source for the union of all Christians in the work of redeeming the world from sin under the leadership and by the authority of the " Strong Son of God, Immortal Love."

CHARLES A. YOUNG.

Chicago, June 7, 1904.

Introduction to the Last Will and Testament of the Springfield Presbytery

BARTON W. STONE was born near Port Tobacco, Maryland, December 24, 1772; while yet an infant he was left fatherless. In 1779 his mother moved to the backwoods of Virginia, near Dan River, Pittsylvania county. "From the time I was able to read I took a great delight in books," but books were scarce in those days, and his means limited; however, he says: "I determined to qualify myself for a barrister, and to acquire a liberal education to accomplish this, I stripped myself of every hindrance, denied myself of strong food and lived chiefly on milk and vegetables, and allowed myself but six or seven hours' sleep out of the twenty-four."

While thus engaged a great religious revival swept over that part of the country. Many of the students of the Academy "got religion," but he would have nothing to do with it, believing it would interfere with his studies. At last he was persuaded to go to hear Mr. James McGready. He was brought under conviction, and after a hard struggle between duty and inclination, finally decided to give up all his cherished plans, his friends, everything, and accept Christ.

This was easier decided on than accomplished. The spirit was willing but he could not *feel* that he was saved. " For a whole year I was tossed on the billows of doubt, laboring, praying, striving to obtain saving faith, sometimes almost despairing of ever getting it." A sermon on " God is love," by William Hodge, finally brought him peace, and when he had studied his Bible alone in the woods, " The great truth finally burst upon me. I yielded, and sank at his feet a willing subject. I loved Him; I adored Him; I praised Him aloud in the silent night in the echoing grove around." This was the turning-point in his life. He now resolved to devote his life to the ministry. " The study of the dead languages became a pleasure." In 1793 he became a candidate for the ministry in the Presbyterian church in Orange county, North Carolina, but before the meeting of the next presbytery changed his mind on account of his inability to reconcile the theological doctrines of the church with the Bible. While in this state of indecision he paid a visit to his brother in Georgia and was chosen Professor of Languages in the Methodist Academy, near Washington. Here he remained for a year, but could not crush out his desire to preach the gospel. He accordingly resigned his position, again applied for license to preach, which was granted. After preaching a short time in Virginia and North Carolina, he, in 1796, made his way through the wilderness to Kentucky, and commenced preaching at Cane Ridge, Bourbon county. His preaching was so acceptable that in the fall of 1798 he received a call to preach for the churches at Cane Ridge and Concord and settle among them.

They were a religious people, and believed the Confession of Faith to be the authorized test of a man's fitness for and right to the Kingdom of God, and those who could not conscientiously subscribe thereto, had no lot nor part with them; brave indeed must be the man who would dare to teach otherwise. The ban of the Presbytery was almost as powerful as the bull of the Pope in the time of Luther. Imagine, then, if you can, what courage it took for the young preacher, who was to follow the eloquent and learned Dr.

Finnley as minister of these churches, when the time came for ordination to call together some of the Presbytery and inform them that he had decided that he could not conscientiously accept this Confession of Faith and would not be ordained. " Doubts had arisen in my mind on the doctrines of election, reprobation and predestination as there taught. Also I stumbled at the doctrine of the Trinity. After laboring in vain to remove my objections and difficulties, they asked me how far I was willing to receive it. I told them, as far as I saw it was consistent with the Word of God. They concluded that was sufficient. I went into the Presbytery, and when the question was proposed, ' Do you receive and adopt the Confession of Faith as containing the system of doctrine taught in the Bible?' I answered aloud, so that the whole congregation might hear, ' I do as far as I see it consistent with the Word of God.' No objection being made, I was ordained."

His work at Cane Ridge and Concord was from the start a great success, but the doubt had entered his soul; not that he doubted God, but that the doctrines of Calvinism he was expected to teach faithfully represented him.

He doubted the system of Calvinism. "How can they believe? How can they repent? How can they do impossibilities? How can they be guilty in not doing them?" To solve these questions he made the Bible his constant companion, and was finally relieved by the precious Word of God. He saw that God did love the world, the whole world, and that the reason men were not saved was because they would not receive the Word of God and believe on his Son."

On July 2, 1801, he married Elizabeth Campbell, of Virginia, and immediately afterwards hurried back to Kentucky to be ready for the camp-meeting, which had been announced to begin the "Thursday or Friday before the third Lord's day in August, 1801." At this meeting a Revolutionary officer estimated that there were 30,000 people in attendance. Take into consideration the population of Kentucky at that time, and you can have some idea of the religious interest that brought so many together. It lasted about seven days and nights, and was discontinued on account of the difficulty in furnishing food for so vast a multitude.

The preaching by the various denominations

during and after the camp-meeting had an un-
expected effect — some began to go away from
the Presbyterian Church to the Methodist and
Baptist. This raised a feeling of alarm in the
ranks of the Ultra-Calvinists, and party lines
were more closely drawn. Objections were
made to the liberal doctrines preached by
Stone, McNemar and others. McNemar's case
was taken up by the Springfield, Ohio, Presbytery, was transferred in 1803 to the Lexington, Kentucky, Synod, and was clearly a test
case. Before the Synod could take action,
five preachers then determined to withdraw,
which they did, and organized the " Springfield
Presbytery." An address to their congregations was prepared setting forth their reasons
for leaving and their objections to the Confession of Faith and "against all authoritative
confessions and creeds founded by fallible
men." " We expressed our total abandonment
of all authoritative creeds but the Bible alone
as the only rule of faith and practice." They
continued to worship under the name of the
Springfield Presbytery, " but we had not worn
our name for more than a year when we saw
it savored of a party spirit. With the man-
made creeds we threw it overboard and took

the name *Christian.*" They then issued the
Last Will and Testament of the Springfield
Presbytery, in which they "*will* that all
names of distinction such as Reverend, etc.,
be forgotten; all delegated authority to make
laws for the church cease; candidates for the
gospel ministry study the *Bible* and obtain
license from God to preach; each particular
congregation to be independent; that the people take the Bible as their only sure guide to
heaven," etc. This was signed by Robert
Marshall, John Dunlavy, Richard McNemar,
B. W. Stone, John Thompson and David Purviance, and dated June 28, 1804. It reminds
us of another remarkable address issued
five years later by Thomas Campbell and
others, in which they agreed to take the
Divine Word alone for "our rule of faith and
practice, the Holy Spirit for our teacher and
guide, and Christ alone, as exhibited in the
Word, for our salvation," and of the motto of
Thomas Campbell, "where the Scriptures speak
we speak; and where the Scriptures are silent,
we are silent." These two movements, so
similar in aim, were destined to become one
in the not distant future.

Once more, farewell.

B W Stone

The Last Will and Testament of the Springfield Presbytery

For where a testament is, there must of necessity be the death of the testator; for a testament is of force after men are dead, otherwise it is of no strength at all, while the testator liveth. Thou fool, that which thou sowest is not quickened except it die. Verily, verily I say unto you, except a corn of wheat fall into the ground, and die, it abideth alone; but if it die, it bringeth forth much fruit. Whose voice then shook the earth; but now he hath promised, saying, yet once more I shake not the earth only, but also heaven. And this word, yet once more, signifies the removing of those things that are shaken as of things that are made, that those things which cannot be shaken may remain.— Scripture.

THE PRESBYTERY OF SPRING-FIELD, sitting at Cane-ridge, in the county of Bourbon, being, through a gracious Providence, in more than ordinary bodily health, growing in strength and size daily; and in perfect soundness and composure of mind; but knowing that it is appointed for all delegated bodies once to die: and considering that the life of every such body is very uncertain, do make, and ordain this our last Will and Testament, in manner and form following, viz.:

Imprimis. We *will,* that this body die, be dissolved, and sink into union with the Body of Christ at large; for there is but one Body, and one Spirit, even as we are called in one hope of our calling.

Item. We *will,* that our name of distinction, with its *Reverend* title, be forgotten, that there be but one Lord over God's heritage, and his name One.

Item. We *will,* that our power of making laws for the government of the church, and executing them by delegated authority, forever cease; that the people may have free course to the Bible, and adopt *the law of the Spirit of life in Christ Jesus.*

Item. We *will,* that candidates for the Gospel ministry henceforth study the Holy Scriptures with fervent prayer, and obtain license from God to preach the simple Gospel, *with the Holy Ghost sent down from heaven,* without any mixture of philosophy, vain deceit, traditions of men, or the rudiments of the world. And let none henceforth take *this honor to himself, but he that is called of God, as was Aaron.*

Item. We *will,* that the church of Christ resume her native right of internal government — try her candidates for the ministry, as to their soundness in the faith, acquaintance with experimental religion, gravity and aptness to teach; and admit no other proof of their authority but Christ speaking in them. We will, that the church of Christ look up to the Lord of the harvest to send forth laborers into his harvest; and that she resume her primitive right of trying those *who say they are apostles, and are not.*

Item. We *will,* that each particular church, as a body, actuated by the same spirit, choose her own preacher, and support him by a free will offering, without a written *call* or *subscription*—admit members—remove offences; and never henceforth *delegate* her right of government to any man or set of men whatever.

Item. We *will,* that the people henceforth take the Bible as the only sure guide to heaven; and as many as are offended with other books, which stand in competition with it, may cast them into the fire if they choose; for it is better to enter into life having one book, than having many to be cast into hell.

Item. We *will,* that preachers and people, cultivate a spirit of mutual forbearance; pray more and dispute less; and while they behold the signs of the times, look up, and confidently expect that redemption draweth nigh.

Item.. We *will,* that our weak brethren, who may have been wishing to make the Presbytery of Springfield their king, and wot not what is now become of it, betake themselves to the Rock of Ages, and follow Jesus for the future.

Item. We *will,* that the Synod of Kentucky examine every member, who may be *suspected* of having departed from the Confession of Faith, and suspend every such suspected heretic immediately; in order that the oppressed may go free, and taste the sweets of gospel liberty.

Item. We *will,* that Ja —— ——, the author of two letters lately published in Lexington, be encouraged in his zeal to destroy *partyism.* We will, moreover, that our past conduct be examined into by all who may have correct information; but let foreigners beware of speaking evil of things which they know not.

Item. Finally we *will,* that all our *sister bodies* read their Bibles carefully, that they may see their fate there determined, and prepare for death before it is too late.

Springfield Presbytery,
June 28th, 1804. } L. S.

ROBERT MARSHALL,
JOHN DUNLAVY,
RICHARD M'NEMAR,
B. W. STONE,
JOHN THOMPSON,
DAVID PURVIANCE, } *Witnesses.*

THE WITNESSES' ADDRESS.

We, the above named witnesses of the **Last Will** and Testament of the Springfield Presbytery, knowing that there will be many conjectures respecting the causes which have occasioned the dissolution of that body, think proper to testify, that from its first existence it was knit together in love, lived in peace and concord, and died a voluntary and happy death.

Their reasons for dissolving that body were

the following: With deep concern they viewed the divisions, and party spirit among professing Christians, principally owing to the adoption of human creeds and forms of government. While they were united under the name of a Presbytery, they endeavored to cultivate a spirit of love and unity with all Christians; but found it extremely difficult to suppress the idea that they themselves were a party separate from others. This difficulty increased in proportion to their success in the ministry. Jealousies were excited in the minds of other denominations; and a temptation was laid before those who were connected with the various parties, to view them in the same light. At their last meeting they undertook to prepare for the press a piece entitled Observations on Church Government, in which the world will see the beautiful simplicity of Christian church government, stript of human inventions and lordly traditions. As they proceeded in the investigation of that subject, they soon found that there was neither precept nor example in the New Testament for such confederacies as modern Church Sessions, Presbyteries, Synods, General Assemblies, etc. Hence

they concluded, that while they continued in
the connection in which they then stood, they
were off the foundation of the Apostles and
Prophets, of which Christ himself is the chief
corner stone. However just, therefore, their
views of church government might have been,
they would have gone out under the name and
sanction of a self-constituted body. Therefore,
from a principle of love to Christians of every
name, the precious cause of Jesus, and dying
sinners who are kept from the Lord by the
existence of sects and parties in the church,
they have cheerfully consented to retire from
the din and fury of conflicting parties — sink
out of the view of fleshly minds, and die the
death. They believe their death will be great
gain to the world. But though dead, as above,
and stript of their mortal frame, which only
served to keep them too near the confines of
Egyptian bondage, they yet live and speak in
the land of gospel liberty; they blow the trumpet of jubilee, and willingly devote themselves
to the help of the Lord against the mighty.
They will aid the brethren, by their counsel,
when required; assist in ordaining elders, or
pastors — seek the divine blessing — unite

with all Christians — commune together, and strengthen each others' hands in the work of the Lord.

We design, by the grace of God, to continue in the exercise of those functions, which belong to us as ministers of the gospel, confidently trusting in the Lord, that he will be with us. We candidly acknowledge, that in some things we may err, through human infirmity; but he will correct our wanderings, and preserve his church. Let all Christians join with us, in crying to God day and night, to remove the obstacles which stand in the way of his work, and give him no rest till he make Jerusalem a praise in the earth. We heartily unite with our Christian brethren of every name, in thanksgiving to God for the display of his goodness in the glorious work he is carrying on in our Western country, which we hope will terminate in the universal spread of the gospel, and the unity of the church.

Introduction to the Declaration and Address

THOMAS CAMPBELL was born in County Down, Ireland, February 1, 1763. His ancestors were Scotch, and several generations before had moved from Scotland to the north of Ireland. From his early years he was of a deeply religious nature, but failed to find satisfaction and peace in the Church of England, to which his father belonged. His brothers belonged to the Seceder Presbyterian Church, and one of them, Archibald, had been a ruling elder for many years in the Seceder Church at Newry, County Down. Thomas was thrown into association with the Seceders and very much preferred their type of religious life and order to that of the Church of England. He put himself under their religious guidance and sought for several years that evidence of an " effectual calling " which was considered by the Seceders to be an indispensable mark of a genuine conversion. He is said to have found the peace he sought through prayerful strivings as he was walking in the fields. He immediately determined to devote his life to the preaching of the Gospel in the Seceder Church.

He had received sufficient education to enable him to teach school in rural places, but not enough to qualify him for service as a minister. He was enabled, through the patronage of a friend, to enter the University of Glasgow, to begin his preparation for the ministry. After completing his course of study at the university he entered the theological school of the Seceders, established and maintained by their synod, at Whithouse. After completing his theological course he was examined by the Presbytery in Ireland, and was licensed to preach as a probationer under the direction of the Synod. He seems not to have been settled in a single parish, but to have followed an itinerary among the weaker churches of a district. He was married in 1787 to Jane Carneigle, near Ballymena, Ireland, where she lived. She was descended from French Huguenots, who fled from France to Ireland at the Revocation of the Edict of Nantes by Louis XIV. To them was born, in 1788, their first child, a son, Alexander, in County Antrim, Ireland.

He continued his work as probationer

among the churches, in connection with his
work as teacher, until 1798. In this year he
was called to become the pastor of the Seceder
Church at Ahorey, a small place four miles
from the city of Armagh. He moved his family to a farm near Rich Hill, about ten miles
from Newry. A little later the family moved
into the town of Rich Hill, where Thomas
Campbell established an academy. While living here the family came into touch with a
congregation of Independents, and was more
or less influenced by them. The Campbells
belonged to the Antiburgher branch of the
Seceder Church, which was characterized as
other branches by a narrow, sectarian spirit.
They were intolerant of other religious bodies
to a degree which made them proverbial for
religious bigotry. They denied the essential
Christian character of other bodies and for-
bade their members on pain of censure or disfellowship to attend their public services, except occasionally when there was no service
in one of their own churches near by. An
instance is recorded of their going so far as
to withdraw fellowship from one of their
members for working as a mason on a chapel
of the Church of England. They regarded the

national churches of England and Scotland as especially antichristian. Such a spirit of narrowness was repulsive to the mind and heart of Thomas Campbell. He availed himself of every privilege of "occasional hearing" at the services of other denominations permitted by his church, and was very friendly with his religious neighbors. The divisions within his own body, the Seceders, seemed trivial, unnecessary and unchristian. In 1804 he led in an effort to unite the Burgher and Antiburgher synods of Ireland. He failed at the time, but it was finally accomplished in 1820, after he had removed to America.

Under the strain of his twofold duties as pastor and teacher his health failed and he was advised to make a journey to America, for the sake of his health and also with the prospect of finding a new home. He left his family in Ireland and made the journey to Philadelphia alone. When he arrived there the synod of his own church was in session. He was at once received upon his testimonials and assigned to pastoral service in western Pennsylvania. He found his brethren in the New World characterized by the same narrowness as his brethren in the Old World. He disregarded their intolerant practices in his pastoral ministrations, and drew upon him the censure of his Presbytery for the exercise of too great Christian liberty and charity toward other religious bodies. It was on this occasion that he wrote the letter to the Synod, to which the case had been appealed. This document, in being the first from his pen in pursuance of his plan of Christian union, is of primary importance as showing the originating conditions, the impelling motive and end of the mission to which he felt himself called from this time on. It will appear that in the year of this episode, 1807-1808, he had firmly grasped the principles of Christian unity set forth at greater length in the " Declaration and Address." He protested against the hasty, unprecedented, and unjustifiable proceedings of the Presbytery of Chartiers," and appealed for reversal of the decision and censure of the course of the Presbytery, to the " Associate Synod of North America." It seems that the Synod removed the censure of the Presbytery in form but reaffirmed it in fact, by holding that there was " sufficient ground to infer censure, and refused to censure the action of the Presbytery according to the demand of

Mr. Campbell. Upon this decision of the Synod he felt obliged to " decline all ministerial connection with, or subjection to, the Associate Synod of North America."

Many friends of Mr. Campbell shared his religious views and sympathized with his course of action. They met and organized themselves into the " Christian Association of Washington," for the purpose of promoting " simple evangelical Christianity, free from all mixture of human opinions and inventions of men." That the public at large might understand the motive and purpose of the Association, Mr. Campbell drew up a statement of their principles and a constitution of the society, called a " Declaration and Address." This is the beginning of one current of that movement which has issued in a community of Christians calling themselves " Christians," or " Disciples of Christ."

ANALYSIS

THE "Declaration and Address" is the product of the spirit and genius of Thomas Campbell. To understand him is to have the key to the explanation of it. To him belongs the credit for the discovery of the principles — if discovery there be — which have contributed more than anything else to the formation of a separate body of Christians calling themselves simply Christians or Disciples of Christ. He coined the great watchwords, "Where the Scriptures speak, we speak; where they are silent, we are silent," a "Thus saith the Lord either in express terms or by approved precedent, for every article of faith, and item of religious practice," "Nothing ought to be received into the faith or worship of the church, or be made a term of communion among Christians, that is not as old as the New Testament," and "The restoration of primitive Christianity."

Thomas Campbell has not received proper appreciation as the real formulator of the principles of the movement. His son arose to a place of leadership by reason of the more popular gifts of oratory and argumentation.

He in no wise surpassed his father in intellectual insight, or originality. It is doubtful if Alexander Campbell added any very important contribution to the principles of the "Declaration and Address." Nearly every important idea or principle may be traced back to the utterances of Thomas Campbell. The son was more bold and aggressive, and possessed the natural gifts of leadership. The father was more retired and less fitted for the stress of combat and opposition that developed at once upon the announcement of the principles of the Association; yet he was the creator, the molding mind and genius of the movement. The testimony of Alexander as to the place of this Address confirms the position taken here. "The Declaration and Address contains what may be called the embryo or the rudiments of a great and rapidly increasing community. It virtually contains the elements of a great movement of vital interest to every citizen of Christ's kingdom."

Thomas Campbell was a man of profound spirituality, Christ-like gentleness and sweetness of spirit, and of a generous nature. He loved God and all men. He longed for the fellowship of all God's people. Sectarianism and division first of all wounded his heart and contradicted his nature; then it was discovered to be contrary to the letter of Scripture. His large heart told him that it was wrong before the Book told him. The discovery that division was contrary to the will of God as expressed in the New Testament touched his gentle spirit into prophetic fervor. Withal his mind was of the highest order of intuitive insight and his speech the most persuasive. His spirit throbs through all the lines of the Address. One has but to imagine the coming together of Seceder Presbyterian sectarianism, bigotry and exclusiveness and Thomas Campbell's catholic and affectionate nature, to account for this document. One must read it with this background in mind.

As will appear from a cursory survey of the document, it is divided into three parts: the " Declaration," which gives the purpose and plan of the Association; the " Address," which goes into a more extended statement of the conditions in the religious world that necessitated such a movement, with a frank avowal of the motives and intentions which actuated them. This is the " Declaration and Address " proper. It is undersigned by

Thomas Campbell and Thomas Acheson. This is followed by an "Appendix" which was designed to "prevent mistakes" and answer objections against the proposed Association and its principles.

I.—PRINCIPLES OF CHRISTIAN UNION

The principles of the Address are unfolded on the lines of the famous maxim of Christian concord enunciated by Meldenius, "Unity in essentials, liberty in non-essentials, charity in all things." While Thomas Campbell expressly rejects this maxim, yet in fact he adopts its essential meaning under the words "faith" and "opinion." They correspond to "essentials" and "non-essentials." The test of essentials and "non-essentials" had been the reason or the decision of councils; he made the express word of Scripture the test, and so preferred the words "faith" and "opinion" as more biblical. All the teaching of the Address may be gathered around these principles. There never was a time when their enunciation was more needed than at the beginning of the Twentieth Century. In the midst of present-day religious unrest and theological transition, we need to admonish the church that there ought to be unity in the things that are essential and need be in nothing else; nay, to reassure her that there is unity therein, and that they are the things that stand sure and steadfast in the midst of all change; that all men should maintain and accord liberty in things not essential; and to preserve charity, love that suffereth long and is kind, in all things.

His contention was two-fold, that there is already unity in essentials, and that there need be unity in nothing else. The essential things were the things expressly enjoined by Scripture as necessary to salvation, and indispensable to the union and communion of the early Christians. These things are plainly taught in the New Testament, and are easily understood by the humblest or youngest Christian disciple. John Wyclif, the great English reformer who anticipated so many principles of the Lutheran reformation, gave utterance to the same thought in the words: "The New Testament is full of authority, and open to the understanding of simple men, as to the points that are most needful to salvation. It seemeth open heresy to say that the gospel with its truth and freedom sufficeth not to salvation of Christian men without keeping of ceremonies and statutes of sinful men."

I.— UNITY IN ESSENTIALS

He clearly shows what he regards as the essentials of Christianity, in his emphasis upon the Lordship of Jesus and the indispensableness of Christian character. He says: " You are all, dear brethren, equally included as the objects of our love and esteem. With you all we desire to unite in the bonds of an entire Christian unity — Christ alone being the head, the center; his word the rule; an explicit belief of, and manifest conformity to it in all things — the terms." He was not concerned with dogmas or doctrines about Christ, but with personal loyalty and likeness to him. He says: " Should this person, moreover, profess that delight and confidence in the Divine Redeemer — that voluntary submission to him — that worship and adoration of him which the Scriptures expressly declare to have been the habits and practice of his people, would not the subject matter of this profession be amply sufficient to impress the believing mind with that dutiful disposition, with that gracious veneration and supreme reverence which the word of God requires? And should not all this taken together satisfy the church, in so far, in point of profession?"

As to the indispensableness of Christian character as a condition of union, he says: "By the Christian church throughout the world, we mean the aggregate of such professors as we have described in Propositions 1 and 8." "It is such only we intend when we urge the necessity of a Christian unity." "A manifest attachment to our Lord Jesus Christ in faith, holiness and charity, was the original criterion of Christian character, the distinguishing badge of our holy profession, the foundation and cement of Christian unity." The emphasis in these passages is evidently upon the manifestation and preservation of a Christian character, Jesus himself being the standard of it. Such only did he contemplate as parties to the union; and only so long as they continued to manifest such character, would they be entitled to fellowship. He regarded a severer discipline in the church as necessary to the preservation of unity. The responsibility for division lay in the reception of persons unfit for Christian fellowship — persons who have not the spirit of Jesus

Christ, his love, his forgiveness, his meekness and forbearance. "We therefore conclude that to advocate unity alone, however desirable in itself, without at the same time purging the church of apparently unsanctified characters, even of all that cannot show their faith by their works, would be, at best, but a poor, superficial, skin-deep reformation."

A distinction is to be made between entering into union with Christians, and the preservation of unity within the Christian community; yet no distinction in the things essential to both. The thing that destroys the unity of the body, disqualifies one for union with it. In other words, no one can be a Christian who cannot live peaceably in fellowship with Christians. All dissocializing elements are unchristian. The Christian virtues are prevailingly social. Christian fellowship thus becomes both a privilege and a probation. The church has been divided and divisions have been perpetuated as much by the unsocial, that is, the unchristian, spirit as by unsound doctrine. If a union of all Christians could be consummated to-day, to-morrow they would be divided, if there was any one a party to the union, who was unloving, unforgiving, unforbearing, disputatious or proud.

2.— LIBERTY IN NON-ESSENTIALS

In his conception the essentials of Christianity were very few, but all-comprehensive; the non-essentials were many, but unimportant. The difficulty arose just here, and ever shall, in distinguishing the essential from the non-essential. He insisted that there was unity among Christians in essentials. Or, to state it reversely, things in which all Christians agree are the essentials. This is but the restatement of that well-known ancient principle, what has been believed always, everywhere, and by all, is the essential faith of the church.

It was felt that this principle was nothing short of the charter of a reunited church. The principle of liberty had been held as a theory in the Protestant church ever since Luther asserted the doctrines of justification by faith, and the right of private interpretation; but really there was little more liberty in the various Protestant bodies than in the Roman Church. The withdrawal of the civil power from the support of the church marked the first great step toward religious liberty. So long as the church and state were united, and the church could invoke the civil power to carry out her decrees, so long was there a kind of unity. But the moment they were separated, the unity that had existed was destroyed, and the church fell apart into a variety of sects. Division was the natural outcome of the Lutheran principles.

The next great step in the progress of the church toward religious liberty is marked — and this is the contribution of Thomas Campbell — by the distinction between the personal faith of the believer and the theological faith of the creeds. With the breaking of the Papal tyranny, there ensued a theological tyranny, which has ruled in the Protestant church through its creeds to the twentieth century. Every new assertion of Christian liberty has resulted in a new tyranny. Luther exercised the greatest liberty of thought personally, but it was lost to his followers. Calvin exercised freedom in the pursuit and acceptance of new truth, but it departed from those who followed him. Thomas Campbell exercised the greatest possible liberty, and would be bound only where the Scriptures bound him; but is it any surprise that there has been less liberty among his followers? Where Luther stopped growing, there Christian thought and life hardened into a fixed form. That which Luther was free to think in his life-time, the next generation was obliged to think, as a condition of fellowship in the Lutheran Church. There is danger that where Thomas and Alexander Campbell arrived in their movement to restore primitive Christianity, there those who gather around them shall stop. The principle of liberty, the right to grow with the growth of truth, needs perpetual emphasis and incessant utterance. Back to this principle has gone every great soul for fresh inspiration and a new starting point in the ascent toward perfect truth as it is in Jesus Christ. Liberty of thought, liberty of opinion, is utterly opposed to authority in opinion. To grant liberty of opinion, liberty in the pursuit of truth, yet to fix beforehand the opinion at which one must arrive, is a denial of liberty.

This principle seems most impossible of application in great transition periods such as the present. The opinions of the last generation of teachers, to which the Campbells belonged, were fixed and definite. They settled the question as to what were mere opinions and what essentials of the faith. To-day there is another set of opinions which has taken their place. The task is laid upon this generation anew to settle the relationship of these opinions to the old, and to the essentials of the faith. The inevitable condition has arrived in which some opinions are pronounced true, others erroneous. It seems the most difficult thing imaginable for those who think the new opinions erroneous, not to go on to judge those opinions dangerous to the faith. Yes, they say, we acknowledge that they are mere opinions, but they are dangerous and ought not to be tolerated. This is an abridgment of liberty in non-essentials.

The conclusion of the whole matter is that there is just as much need of liberty in new opinion as in old opinion with which adjustment has been reached. In other words, openness to new truth, new ideas, new opinions, is just as essential to the unity of the church as liberty in old opinion. The refusal of the teachers of the church to be hospitable toward new truth has driven some of her best spirits from her, and obliged them to form new organizations for fellowship. The church of the very next generation has frequently welcomed truth that was rejected by the preceding. There are new truths being uttered to-day, which, though denied a place in the body of Christian truth by the church of to-day, will become a part of it to-morrow. There are new sects arising every year and building upon rejected truth — truth for which the existing churches have found no place.

3.— CHARITY IN ALL THINGS

If men are to be accorded liberty to think, they must be accorded liberty to differ. Where such differences arise, there is need of the utmost charity. The things that saddened and pained the soul of Thomas Campbell were the criminations and recriminations going on between brethren in the Church over differences of opinion. Nothing seemed farther from the spirit of the Christian, nothing so completely negatived the Christian character, as uncharitable condemnation of a brother with whom one differed. He enumerates three evils which seem to him to be especially heinous: " First, to determine expressly, in the name of the Lord, when the Lord has not expressly determined, appears to us a very great evil." " A second evil is, not only judging our brother to be absolutely wrong, because he differs from our opinions, but more especially our judging him to be a transgressor of the law in so doing, and, of course, treating him as such by censuring or otherwise exposing him to contempt, or, at least, preferring ourselves before him in our judgment, saying, as it were, ' Stand by; I am holier than thou.' " This evil of bringing a brother into contempt whose ideas we do not like is a favorite method with those who have no severer pains they can inflict. It is one in spirit and purpose with the medieval Inquisition which could inflict the pain of confiscation of goods or even death. It results to-day frequently that a brother can be made to suffer in his goods by injuring his reputation for soundness in the faith; for many a teacher is entirely dependent upon this for his acceptance among a religious people. Causing a brother any slightest pain of body or mind on account of difference of opinion is utterly contrary to the spirit of this great principle, and subversive of the unity of the Church. But when the early Protestants could not inflict pain upon the body of a heretic, they pursued this other method of sinister and invidious undermining of his good name as a means of showing him the truth.

The defense of religious controversy is often made on the ground that liberty in non-essentials is not intended to abridge the right or the need of discussion of doctrines or opinions. Campbell himself acknowledged the place of friendly comparison of views as a means to the discovery of truth. One may even go so far as to " declare that, in our judgment, our brother is in error, which we may sometimes do in a perfect consistence with charity;" but he did reprobate the arrogance and assumed superiority which led one to deny the right of a brother to confidence and fellowship because of difference of opinion.

" A third and still more dreadful evil is, when we not only, in this kind of way, judge and set at naught our brother, but, moreover, proceed as a church acting and judging in the name of Christ, not only to determine that our brother is wrong because he differs from our determination, but also, in connection with this proceed so far as to determine the merits of the cause by rejecting or casting him out of the church as unworthy of a place in her communion, and thus, as far as in our power, cutting him off from the kingdom of Heaven." His entire treatment of this matter is both suggestive and timely. He anticipates another apology for this sort of excommunication in the words: "If, after all, any particular church acting thus should refuse the foregoing conclusion, by saying, we meant no such thing concerning the person rejected (that is, exclusion from the benefits of the kingdom), we only judged him unworthy of a place among us, but there are other churches that may receive him"—his response is in substance: If the other church that receives the rejected brother is a church of Christ by acknowledgment, then it has condemned the action of the church that rejected him, and that church in turn condemns the one that received him. What is this but to invite division and strife into the church?

That Thomas Campbell entertained the most charitable and brotherly sentiments toward those Christians with whom he differed in opinion is evident from his kindly appeals to them as brethren to enter with him into the work of bringing the churches together. "Our brethren of all denominations," "Our dear brethren," "Dearly beloved brethren," "All the churches of Christ," are phrases recurrent on almost every page of the Address. Consistent with these professions of Christian regard for all the churches is his readiness to join with them in the laudable work of reformation. " But this we do sincerely declare that there is nothing we have hitherto received as matter of faith or practice which is not expressly taught or enjoined in the word of God, either in express terms or approved precedent, that we would not heartily relinquish, that so we might return to the original constitutional unity of the Christian Church; and in this happy unity, enjoy full communion with all our brethren, in peace and charity."

II.—PLAN OF CHRISTIAN UNION

The doctrine of Christian union as set forth in the Address may be summarized as follows:

(1) The church, the body of Christ, is divided into warring factions.

(2) Such divisions in the church of Christ are unscriptural, unnecessary and wrong.

(3) The church is divided on account of its departure from the authority and teaching of the New Testament: the substitution of human tests of fellowship for the divine;

devotion to human leaders and names instead of the one great Leader, Jesus; the confusing of merely human opinion with the essential faith as a requirement of salvation.

(4) The church of apostolic times was essentially one.

(5) The church may be reunited by a return to the divine standard and conformity thereto in all things.

1. It appears from the document that the *bond* of union was to be a common authority, the New Testament, or the teaching of Jesus and the apostles. He saw the need, first of all, of an authority to which all Christians would bow, as the essential condition of any enduring union. The question of authority conditioned the entire enterprise. He found in the New Testament an authority which all the churches acknowledged. This was the fundamental starting point. It is embodied in the motto, "Where the Scriptures speak, we speak; where they are silent, we are silent." This motto fixes two things, the seat of authority in religion and the limits of religious liberty.

2. The *basis* of union was to be the conditions of union or fellowship with Christ, as

set forth in the New Testament. His plan was to ignore the intervening history of the church, with its corruptions, and begin where the apostles left off. The fundamental assumption of their preaching was to be that there had been no time since Pentecost. Hence the basis of union for the divided church was to be identical with the New Testament conditions of personal union with Christ. It contemplated every denomination as a single individual Christian. He had no thought of a concordat, or articles of association for churches, other than for individual Christians. With him organizations of the various sects, their forms, systems and governments had no essential existence. After all, relation to Christ is personal, not congregational or denominational, no more than national; and there can be no Christian union except of those in Christ. Those who are in Christ are essentially one, but are separated by unscriptural and human inventions. He had no plan for an ecclesiastical league. He had no thought of an alliance or confederacy of various institutions into a league of peace, but of a union of Christians.

3. The *form* of the union was to be " an

entire union of all the churches in faith and practice according to the Word of God." He does not go beyond this general outline to specify the things that are to be believed or practiced, assuming that when once the principle of the sufficiency of the divine standard and model — the church of the New Testament — has been accepted, and men begin to inquire in its pages as to what is the will of God concerning his church, they will all at once fall upon the same self-evident truths of faith and practice. Then will follow a reduction of all existing church systems to " that whole form of doctrine, worship, discipline and government, expressly revealed and enjoined in the Word of God." Nothing would satisfy his conception but one church as in apostolic times, which however, " must necessarily exist in particular and distinct societies, locally separate from one another." A union which does not reduce the many sects to the one primitive church — a union which leaves out of its fellowship one true Christian or makes it impossible for one who is a Christian according to the Scriptural requirement to become a member in it — is not an entire Christian unity. His conception of the church governed

his idea of its unity. He says, Prop. 1: "That
the Church of Christ upon earth is essentially,
intentionally and constitutionally one; consisting of all those in every place that profess
their faith in Christ and obedience to him in
all things according to the Scriptures, and that
manifest the same by their tempers and conduct." Such was the church of apostolic times.
There was unity without external enforcement,
difference of opinion without disfellowship;
many churches scattered through many lands,
composed of many races, but "one Lord, one
faith, one baptism." A member of one local
church was welcome to the membership of
every other church. Thus ought it to be now.

Such a union will be visible and universal,
but not formal, for it will grow out of vital
relation to Christ, and all that are in him will
be in fellowship with each other here on earth.
It will embrace no more, no less. All other
forms or schemes of union, upon any other
plan, will inevitably leave out some one who
simply belongs to Christ. He sought to make
the visible church coextensive with the spiritual
church — the one exactly covering and filling
the other. To accomplish this end, " nothing
ought to be inculcated upon Christians as

articles of faith, nor required of them as terms of communion, but what is expressly taught and enjoined upon them in the Word of God." The Christian profession should describe the Christian reality.

4. His *program* was as simple as his basis. This union was to be accomplished by sending out preachers to proclaim the principle among the churches. The Association was not a church but "merely voluntary advocates for church reformation." The members were to retain their membership in their respective denominational churches. They expected to be received cordially into all the churches on an interdenominational mission. Just as to-day the "Woman's Christian Temperance Union" is a society for the promotion and unification of the temperance sentiment among the churches, so Thomas Campbell thought of this movement. How suddenly all doors were closed to him, and he was obliged to alter his program, seeking first to merge the movement with the Presbyterians, and finally merging it with the Baptists, has been recorded in the Introduction. Gradually those who adopted the principles of the Address among the Baptists became distinguished in all Bap-

tist churches from orthodox Baptists. With the development of hostility between these two elements there came a period of division, which resulted in the complete separation of the "Reforming Baptists" from the "Regular Baptists." The former body took the name "Disciples of Christ" or "Christians," but were in various sections nicknamed "Campbellites." It must be apparent to every one who has followed the history of this body to the present time how different have been the issues and fortunes of the movement, as compared with the original purpose and program of the author of this document.

The circumstances which gave rise to the movement, the spirit which animated its leaders, the principles underlying their pronunciamento, classify it as a Christian union movement. They thought the reunion of Protestant churches would be an immediate realization upon the principles set forth. They discovered to their disappointment that the denominations were not ready to lay down their differences at the first suggestion. They found that there was very much ground to be cleared before the end in view could be directly worked at. They were set for the union of all Christians, but the task of preparing the way for it was first in order and proved more serious. Hence they were thrown back upon the discussion and defense of the basis of union — namely, primitive Christianity, what it is and how to interpret it. Common agreement has not yet been reached as to what it is in all of its essential elements. There are evidences, however, of a growing agreement as to the sufficiency, nay, the exclusive right, of primitive Christianity to be the basis of a reunited church. The desirability of union is acknowledged on all hands.

The Declaration and Address is essentially a Christian union document and belongs to the literature of the subject. It takes a place beside such documents as, " Tract on Union Among Christians," by John Owen; " True and Only Way of Concord of All Christian Churches," by Richard Baxter, and similar treatises by George Calixtus, Hugo Grotius and the philosopher Leibnitz. A brief survey of the chief attempts at union since the Reformation will help us to understand the Declaration and Address.

The inevitable result of the acceptance of the principles of the Reformation was division and sectarianism. No sooner did they see the mistake and weakness of division than they began to seek some basis for reunion. Before Luther's death there were various attempts at union. After his death they were renewed with greater earnestness. Lutheran and Catholic, Reformed and Lutheran, were now and again holding conferences over some consensus or concordat. It will suffice to pass in review only a few important efforts and proposals.

George Calixtus (1586-1666) led one of the earliest and most earnest efforts to reunite the Protestants and Catholics. He proposed that they go back to the creeds of the first five centuries of the church as the doctrinal basis of union. He held "That the fundamental doctrines of Christianity, sufficient for salvation, were contained in the Apostles' Creed, and in the common faith, explanatory thereof, of the first five centuries." In the main features of his proposal he followed Cassander. His basis of union may be designated as confessio-theological; that is, the basis of agreement is to be found in the doctrines of the early creeds or confessions, which are essentially theological.

These principles were adopted and set forth by Leibnitz (1646-1716) in renewed efforts to effect a union between Protestants and Catholics. He was met on the side of the Catholics by Spinola and Bossuet. He met with such success at Hanover in 1683, in a conference with these men, that an agreement seemed imminent. It was under these circumstances that, in 1686, Leibnitz wrote his " System of Theology," in which he strove to find common standing ground for Protestants and Catholics in the details of their creeds. When it was discovered that the Catholic theologians were seeking not a compromise with the Protestants, but their conversion, the correspondence was dropped. He took the conciliar decrees of the first three centuries as the doctrinal basis of the union. The Catholics insisted on the decrees of the Council of Trent in addition.

Lessing, the German dramatist, the father and master of literary criticism, was directed late in life to a study of theology. He was led to ask himself the question, " What is essential to Christianity? " He contended that Christianity was older than the Bible, hence the New Testament was not absolutely necessary to Christianity. He adopted the view of an "essential Christ" of all ages and peoples, back of all creeds and history. He identified Christianity with noble character. This was his basis of union for all the world, Protestant, Catholic, Jew, and Mohammedan alike. They were all agreed as to the essential nobility of character. This may be called a naturo-ethical basis.

Grotius of the Reformed Church of the Netherlands was occupied many years with a program of union between Protestant and Catholic bodies. "The differences among Christians appeared to him small compared with the points on which they were united." He spent many years in close conference with the Catholic leaders in France. Grotius advocated a general council of Protestants and Catholics as the only means of arriving at a consensus of doctrine. The basis which he proposed was likewise a theological one.

All these proposals agree in starting with something the parties to the union could acknowledge as of binding authority. The tendency was to go back toward the early symbols of the faith of the church to find a common ground on which to stand together.

None proposed going back so far as Thomas
Campbell. The difference between Campbell
and his predecessors in this effort for union
is apparent. Campbell's basis was not theological or ethical, nor did it center around
a creed or council; it was Biblico-ethical and
Christo-centric.

III.—PRESUPPOSITIONS

The Declaration and Address was put forth
with a view to its acceptance by a certain part
of the religious world. Thomas Campbell did
not anticipate any response from Roman
Catholics or Unitarians. He stood upon
ground he believed common to the great
majority of evangelical Protestants. There
were therefore some things assumed as commonly agreed upon, underlying the Address —
some things that did not seem to be debatable
between them. These commonly accepted,
self-evident truths, of which he speaks, are
what give to the overture such a buoyancy
of hope, confident expectancy, and almost
prophetic assurance of success. He says:
" We might further add, that the attempt here
suggested not being of a partial, but of a
general nature, it can have no just tendency

to excite the jealousy, or hurt the feelings of any party. On the contrary, every effort toward a permanent Scriptural unity among the churches, upon the solid basis of universally acknowledged and self-evident truths, must have the happiest tendency to enlighten and conciliate, by thus manifesting to each other their mutual charity and zeal for the truth." Of these universally acknowledged and self-evident truths which constituted the common basis for Christian union, the following seem the most important and apparent:

1. *The Scriptures of the New Testament are the supreme and ultimate source of authority for Christian faith and practice.*

The ever recurrent appeal in the Address is to the Scriptures — a " Thus saith the Lord for every article of faith or item of religious practice." This is no less than the formal principle of the Protestant Reformation. It will be observed that he distinguishes the authority of the New Testament from that of the Old. Proposition 4 of the Address reads as follows: "That although the Scriptures of the Old and New Testaments are inseparably connected, making together but one perfect and entire revelation of the Divine will, for the edification and salvation of the Church, and therefore in that respect cannot be separated; yet as to what directly and properly belongs to their immediate object, the New Testament is as perfect a constitution for the worship, discipline and government of the New Testament Church, and as perfect a rule for the particular duties of its members, as the Old Testament was for the worship, discipline, and government of the Old Testament Church, and the particular duties of its members." Here lie the germs of that distinction between the old and new covenants, which subsequently became so important in the teaching of Alexander Campbell.

2. *That the New Testament contains a perfect and complete model of the Christian institution, as to faith, life, worship, ordinances, and government.*

The evident meaning of such exhortations as, "conform to the model," "conform to the original pattern laid down in the New Testament," is that Jesus and the apostles anticipated every need, and provided for every exigency in the career of the church on earth, before they passed away. Those provisions have been preserved for us in the New Testament. In other words, nothing was left to the church to devise, and no liberty was allowed the church to alter those things already devised. As the ordinances were observed by Jesus and the apostles, so were they to be observed forever in the church. As the church was organized by the apostles, with elders and deacons, so was it always to be organized to the end of its existence on earth.

3. *That the Scriptures are essentially and intentionally intelligible, as far as matters of salvation are concerned.* The right of private interpretation is assumed on every page, as well as the certainty that all who read the Scriptures without preconceptions, will come to the same understanding of them. The things that concern one's salvation are plain and simple. They must be so, else the church would be a place for none but the learned; but it has ever consisted of " little children and young men, as well as fathers." The Scriptures therefore do not permit of a double or doubtful meaning. He says: " Should it be still further objected that all these sects and many more profess to believe the Bible, to believe it to be the Word of God, and, therefore, will readily profess to believe and prac-

tice whatever is revealed and enjoined therein, and yet each will understand it his own way, and of course practice accordingly; nevertheless, according to the plan proposed, you receive them all. We would ask, then, do all these profess and practice neither more nor less than what we read in the Bible, than what is expressly revealed and enjoined therein? If so, they all profess and practice the same thing, for the Bible exhibits but one and the self-same thing to all."

4. *That the church needs reforming by being restored to the New Testament model, and that a complete restoration is both desirable and possible.* There was probably less agreement among the churches as to the last two than the first two presuppositions. There was serious doubt of both the desirability and possibility of restoring the primitive church. This, however, was the firm conviction of Thomas Campbell, that the divided condition of the church is perfectly hopeless on any other basis. To Campbell's mind the sufficiency of the apostolic model grew naturally and consistently out of the authority of Scripture. To the Protestant churches of that day, the authority of Scripture was one thing, the

sufficiency and fitness of the primitive church as a model for the church of all times was another thing.

5. *That the church of apostolic times was essentially and intentionally one organic body.* This is expressed in so many words in the first proposition of the Address, and in the frequently occurring phrase, " The original constitutional unity of the primitive church."

6. *That matters of faith and opinion in Christianity are easily distinguishable, and that recognition of what is thus essential and what is non-essential will result in unity of faith and practice.* All Christians agreed that there was a difference between faith and opinion, but where to draw the line, and what to put on one side, and what on the other side, was not so easily settled. Campbell went no further in the classification of faith and opinions than to say that matters of faith were those things expressly enjoined by the Word of God as necessary to salvation, while private opinions were inferences or deductions from them.

7. *That the apostles stood upon the same plain of infallibility and authority in their teaching as that on which Jesus stood.* This question had not been raised in the year 1809.

A distinction between the authority and value of the Old and New Testaments had not been made until the Campbells began to make it. The entire Bible was looked upon as a single revelation of God, each part equally valuable and authoritative for the Christian. The question of a difference of value between the writings of the New Testament is a late nineteenth century question.

These are the presuppositions upon which Thomas Campbell founded his confidence in the possibility of restoring unity to a large part of Christendom. These principles have been quietly assumed in most of the teaching and preaching of the Disciples of Christ. Since the writing of the Address those who gave in their adherence to it have gone on to define primitive Christianity in the concrete, and to fill in the content. In the Address it is merely an outline, a principle, a plan of action. The task of defining primitive Christianity was inevitably forced upon them. All parties might agree and doubtless did agree, that primitive Christianity is an authoritative and sufficient model; but, "What is primitive Christianity," would be sure to be the first question raised.

Differences arose at once and still continue among the supporters of the Declaration and Address as to the essential elements of primitive Christianity. More or less latitude has been exercised in the practical work of reproducing the primitive model. Some have been more strict than others in the interpretation of the principle. Some have maintained that the essential elements of primitive Christianity extend to details of time, place, and season of observing the ordinances; to custom, order, and furniture of public worship; to method and plan of missionary activity; to names and function of service in the church. We find accordingly, those who regard the use of modern instruments of music in public worship as a violation of primitive precept and example. Missionary societies, Christian Endeavor societies, Sunday schools, prayer meetings, trustees, pastors, hymn books and a multitude of other modern helps, have each in turn been opposed as violations of the principle. Who shall construe for us the exact meaning of primitive Christianity? Who shall fix infallibly the application of the principle to the varying exigencies of the times? The Disciples have settled down to the exercise of the greatest liberty consistent with the Christian spirit.

As there is difference among the Disciples concerning the interpretation and application of this principle, so is there with respect to all of these presuppositions. The practical question to-day is not whether there was general agreement in these principles in 1809, but whether there is general agreement in them in 1904. It may be confidently asserted that they do not precisely represent present-day Christian thought. But since it is not within the scope of this historical study to interpret the thought and attitude of the church of to-day toward them, it will suffice to indicate the presence here of an important inquiry. Are the Disciples entirely satisfied with the achievements of nearly one hundred years of advocacy of Christian union? Are they ready to fight it out on these lines if it takes a millennium? As a Christian union program are these principles a success? Have they been faithfully interpreted and applied? As an evangelistic force, as fishers of men, as founders of churches upon the primitive model, all men agree that the success of the Disciples has been signal. But besides having a mission as a church of Christ, which is to seek and save the lost, the Disciples have clung to another special mission as a society for the promotion of Christian union, growing out of their attachment to the Declaration and Address. This inquiry refers solely to the historic mission of the Disciples, not to their mission as simply Christians, which they have in common with all Christians. The Declaration and Address was put forth before the Christian Association of Washington was compelled to constitute itself into a regular church. That Association was not a church in any sense at the time of the writing of this Address; it was the constitution of a Christian union and church reformation society. It did not lose its purpose as a society when it became a church.

your affectionate Father –

Thomas Campbell

Declaration and Address*

FROM the series of events which have taken place in the churches for many years past, especially in this Western country, as well as from what we know in general of the present state of things in the Christian world, we are persuaded that it is high time for us not only to think, but also to act, for ourselves; to see with our own eyes, and to take all our measures directly and immediately from the Divine standard; to this alone we feel ourselves Divinely bound to be

* This "Declaration and Address" was not the constitution of any Church existing then or now, but a "Declaration" of a purpose to institute a society of "Voluntary Advocates for Church Reformation." Its sole purpose was to promote "simple Evangelical Christianity," and for this end resolved to countenance and support such ministers, and such only, as exhibited a manifest conformity to the original standard, in conversation, doctrine, zeal, and diligence; such as practiced that simple, original form of Christianity expressly exhibited upon the sacred page; without inculcating anything of human authority, of private opinion, or of inventions of men, as having any place in the constitution, faith, or worship of the Christian Church; or anything as matter of Christian faith or duty for which there cannot be expressly produced a "*Thus saith the Lord, either in express terms, or by approved precedent.*"

conformed, as by this alone we must be judged. We are also persuaded that as no man can be *judged* for his brother, so no man can *judge* for his brother; every man must be allowed to judge for himself, as every man must bear his own judgment — must give account of himself to God. We are also of opinion that as the Divine word is equally binding upon all, so all lie under an equal obligation to be bound by it, and it alone; and not by any human interpretation of it; and that, therefore, no man has a right to judge his brother, except in so far as he manifestly violates the express letter of the law. That every such judgment is an express violation of the law of Christ, a daring usurpation of his throne, and a gross intrusion upon the rights and liberties of his subjects. We are, therefore, of opinion that we should beware of such things; that we should keep at the utmost distance from everything of this nature; and that, knowing the judgment of God against them that commit such things, we should neither do the same ourselves, nor take pleasure in them that do them. Moreover, being well aware, from sad experience, of the heinous nature and pernicious tendency of religious controversy among

Declaration and Address

Christians; tired and sick of the bitter jarrings and janglings of a party spirit, we would desire to be at rest; and, were it possible, we would also desire to adopt and recommend such measures as would give rest to our brethren throughout all the churches: as would restore unity, peace, and purity to the whole Church of God. This desirable rest, however, we utterly despair either to find for ourselves, or to be able to recommend to our brethren, by continuing amid the diversity and rancor of party contentions, the veering uncertainty and clashings of human opinions: nor, indeed, can we reasonably expect to find it anywhere but in Christ and his simple word, which is the same yesterday, to-day, and forever. Our desire, therefore, for ourselves and our brethren would be, that, rejecting human opinions and the inventions of men as of any authority, or as having any place in the Church of God, we might forever cease from further contentions about such things; returning to and holding fast by the original standard; taking the Divine word alone for our rule; the Holy Spirit for our teacher and guide, to lead us into all truth; and Christ alone, as exhibited in the word, for our salvation; that, by so

73

doing, we may be at peace among ourselves, follow peace with all men, and holiness, without which no man shall see the Lord. Impressed with these sentiments, we have resolved as follows:

I.   That we form ourselves into a religious association under the denomination of the Christian Association of Washington, for the sole purpose of promoting simple evangelical Christianity, free from all mixture of human opinions and inventions of men.

II.   That each member, according to ability, cheerfully and liberally subscribe a certain specified sum, to be paid half yearly, for the purpose of raising a fund to support a pure Gospel ministry, that shall reduce to practice that whole form of doctrine, worship, discipline, and government, expressly revealed and enjoined in the word of God.   And, also, for supplying the poor with the holy Scriptures.

III.   That this Society consider it a duty, and shall use all proper means in its power, to encourage the formation of similar associations; and shall for this purpose hold itself in readiness, upon application, to correspond with, and render all possible assistance to, such as may desire to associate for the same desirable and important purposes.

IV. That this Society by no means considers itself a Church, nor does at all assume to itself the powers peculiar to such a society; nor do the members, as such, consider themselves as standing connected in that relation; nor as at all associated for the peculiar purposes of Church association; but merely as voluntary advocates for Church reformation; and, as possessing the powers common to all individuals, who may please to associate in a peaceable and orderly manner, for any lawful purpose, namely, the disposal of their time, counsel and property, as they may see cause.

V. That this Society, formed for the sole purpose of promoting simple evangelical Christianity, shall, to the utmost of its power, countenance and support such ministers, and such only, as exhibit a manifest conformity to the original standard in conversation and doctrine, in zeal and diligence; only such as reduce to practice that simple original form of Christianity, expressly exhibited upon the sacred page; without attempting to inculcate anything of human authority, of private opinion, or inventions of men, as having any place in the constitution, faith, or worship, of the Christian Church, or anything as matter of Christian faith or duty, for which there can not be expressly produced a " Thus saith the Lord, either in express terms, or by approved precedent." *

VI. That a Standing Committee of twenty-one members of unexceptionable moral character, inclusive of the secretary and treasurer, be chosen annually to superintend the interests, and transact the business of the Society. And that said Committee be invested with full powers to act and do, in the name and behalf of their constituents, whatever the Society had previously determined, for the purpose of

* On reading the proof-sheets of this " Declaration," as they issued from the press, immediately after my arrival in Washington, Pennsylvania, direct from Scotland, I observed to its author: " *Then, sir, you must abandon and give up infant baptism, and some other practices for which it seems to me you cannot produce an express precept or an example in any book of the Christian Scriptures!* "

After a considerable pause, his response was to this effect: " *To the law and to the testimony* " we *make our appeal. If not* found therein, we, of course, must abandon it. But, he added: " we could not unchurch ourselves now, and go out into the world and then turn back again and enter the Church, merely for the sake of form or decorum."

But, we replied, if there be any virtue, privilege,

carrying into effect the entire object of its institution, and that in case of any emergency, unprovided for in the existing determinations of the Society, said Committee be empowered to call a special meeting for that purpose.

VII. That this Society meet at least twice a year, viz.: on the first Thursday of May, and of November, and that the collectors appointed to receive the half-yearly quotas of the promised subscriptions, be in readiness, at or before each meeting, to make their returns to the treasurer, that he may be able to report upon the state of the funds. The next meeting to be held at Washington on the first Thursday of November next.

or blessing in submitting to any ordinance, of course we cannot enjoy that virtue, privilege, or blessing, whatever it may be, of which it is an ordained, a Divinely appointed instrumentality or medium. "Without faith it is impossible to please God" in any act, or in any formal obedience to any precept, ordinance, or institution; and equally true that without this faith we cannot enjoy any act of obedience to either a moral, a positive, or a religious ordinance of any class whatever. There is a promised reward, or, rather an immediate blessing, attendant on every act of obedience to the Divine precepts; and, as you have taught, "the blessings attached to, or connected with the moral *positive,* are superior to those connected with the moral *natural."* And, as for an assent to an opinion, there is no virtue in it.

[ALEXANDER CAMPBELL.]

VIII. That each meeting of the Society be opened with a sermon, the constitution and address read, and a collection lifted for the benefit of the Society; and that all communications of a public nature be laid before the Society at its half-yearly meetings.

IX. That this Society, relying upon the all-sufficiency of the Church's Head; and, through his grace, looking with an eye of confidence to the generous liberality of the sincere friends of genuine Christianity; holds itself engaged to afford a competent support to such ministers as the Lord may graciously dispose to assist, at the request, and by invitation of the Society, in promoting a pure evangelical reformation, by the simple preaching of the everlasting Gospel, and the administration of its ordinances in an exact conformity to the Divine standard as aforesaid; and that, therefore, whatever the friends of the institution shall please to contribute toward the support of ministers in connection with this Society, who may be sent forth to preach at considerable distances, the same shall be gratefully received and acknowledged as a donation to its funds.

ADDRESS, Etc.

To all that love our Lord Jesus Christ, in sincerity, throughout all the Churches, the following Address is most respectfully submitted.

DEARLY BELOVED BRETHREN:

That it is the grand design and native tendency of our holy religion to reconcile and unite men to God, and to each other, in truth and love, to the glory of God, and their own present and eternal good, will not, we presume, be denied, by any of the genuine subjects of Christianity. The nativity of its Divine author was announced from heaven, by a host of angels, with high acclamations of " Glory to God in the highest, and on earth peace and good-will toward men." The whole tenor of that Divine book which contains its institutes, in all its gracious declarations, precepts, ordinances, and holy examples, most expressively and powerfully inculcates this. In so far, then, as this holy unity and unanimity in faith and love is attained, just in the same degree is the glory of God and the happiness of men promoted and secured. Impressed with those

79

sentiments, and, at the same time, grievously affected with those sad divisions which have so awfully interfered with the benign and gracious intention of our holy religion, by exciting its professed subjects to bite and devour one another, we cannot suppose ourselves justifiable in withholding the mite of our sincere and humble endeavors to heal and remove them.

What awful and distressing, effects have those sad divisions produced! what aversions, what reproaches, what backbitings, what evil surmisings, what angry contentions, what enmities, what excommunications, and even persecution!!! And, indeed, this must, in some measure, continue to be the case so long as those schisms exist; for, saith the apostle, where envying and strife is, *there* is confusion and every evil work. What dreary effects of those accursed divisions are to be seen, even in this highly favored country, where the sword of the civil magistrate has not as yet learned to serve at the altar. Have we not seen congregations broken to pieces, neighborhoods of professing Christians first thrown into confusion by party contentions, and, in the end, entirely deprived of Gospel ordinances;

while, in the mean time, large settlements and tracts of country remain to this day entirely destitute of a Gospel ministry, many of them in little better than a state of heathenism, the Churches being either so weakened with divisions that they cannot send them ministers, or the people so divided among themselves that they will not receive them. Several, at the same time, who live at the door of a preached Gospel, dare not in conscience go to hear it, and, of course, enjoy little more advantage, in that respect, than if living in the midst of heathens. How seldom do many in those circumstances enjoy the dispensations of the Lord's Supper, that great ordinance of unity and love. How sadly, also, does this broken and confused state of things interfere with that spiritual intercourse among Christians, one with another, which is so essential to their edification and comfort, in the midst of a present evil world; so divided in sentiment, and, of course, living at such distances, that but few of the same opinion,* or party, can

* "*Opinions*" were, in those days, and even yet are very popular in the pulpits and in the presses of religious sectaries of all the denominational religions of the living world. Yet the word "*opinion*" is not once found in the Christian Scriptures, nor

conveniently and frequently assemble for religious purposes, or enjoy a due frequency of

even in the Jewish records, except once by Elijah, in a case pending between the worshipers of Baal and those of Jehovah. No man ever *believed* an *opinion* or a *doctrine!* He may assent to them, but to *believe* an *opinion* or a *doctrine* is simply absurd.

The discriminating reason has to do with *opinions.* They are tried by *reasoning* upon them, pro or con. Hence, they are debatable alone in the court of reason. But faith has to do with *testimony,* as hope has to do with a *promise,* and fear with a *threatening.* We *believe,* when reported, well-authenticated facts and events. We *hope* in promises believed. We *fear and tremble* at threatenings enunciated. We *obey* precepts when propounded, and not before, and only when they emanate from legitimate authority.

Such is a practical view of the constitution of the human mind, as God created it. And such is the well-authenticated meaning of these words in the currency of those who properly appreciate and understand our language.

The corrupt language of Ashdod has fearfully invaded the pulpit and the press of the living world. It is well illustrated in Nehemiah, chapter xii, in his history of the Jewish captivity. One passage will suffice: "In those days also, I saw Jews who had married wives of Ashdod, of Ammon, and of Moab. And their children *spoke half in the speech of Ashdod, and could not speak in the Jewish language;* but, according to the language of each people." "And," says Nehemiah the reformer, "I contended with them and reviled them."

Babylon the great, is the antitype of old Babylon. And most Protestants that have come out of her still speak, and preach, and teach in a mixed and confused dialect.

No one of Elder Campbell's contemporaries known to me more earnestly contended and labored than he

ministerial attentions. And even where things
are in a better state with respect to settled

for "a pure speech," a Scriptural dialect, or the
calling of Bible *themes* by Bible names. "The
restoration of a pure speech" was with him a
cardinal theme, and a petition in many a prayer.

How many debates, schisms, and alienations of
heart and life have grown out of "the articles of
faith," or "the doctrines" of the present generation.
"Doctrines," like "articles of faith," are wholly
uncanonical. In the Christian Scriptures we never
read of the "doctrines of Christ." It is always
singular, never plural. "Doctrines," like "articles
of faith," are unprecedented in the New Testament,
except in the case of *demons,* and those under their
influence. And how many more in the generations
past and gone! According to the apostolic style the
Christian faith is called "*The doctrine of Christ,*"
and all other faiths or theories are called "the
doctrines of men," or "of demons."

There is a pride of opinion more subtile, and more
permeating the religious world than is generally supposed or imagined. A zeal wholly sectarian and
selfish is more easily detected in others than in
ourselves. Our premises and our observations of
the religious world, for at least one-half a century,
more than justify this opinion.

The strength or *spiritual power* of the apostolic
Gospel is now, has been heretofore, and will, till
time shall end, continue to be, "the power of God
to salvation," to every one who clearly appreciates
and embraces it in his affections, and consequently
acts in harmony with its spiritual and eternal obligations. Indeed, we cannot conceive of higher claims
and demand on the heart, the life, the devotion of
man to his Creator and Redeemer, than are found
in the doctrine of Christ, duly appreciated and
cordially embraced.

It presents to us transcendent facts to be believed,

83

Churches, how is the tone of discipline relaxed under the influence of a party spirit; many being afraid to exercise it with due strictness, lest their people should leave them, and, under the cloak of some specious pretense, find refuge in the bosom of another party; while, lamentable to be told, so corrupted is the Church with those accursed divisions, that there are but few so base as not to find admission into some professing party or other. Thus, in a great measure, is that Scriptural purity of communion banished from the Church of God, upon the due preservation of which much of her comfort, glory, and usefulness depend. To complete the dread result of our woful divisions, one evil yet remains, of a very awful nature: the Divine displeasure justly provoked with this sad perversion of the Gospel of peace, the Lord withholds his

precepts to be obeyed, threatenings to be feared, promises to be hoped for, and an ineffably beautiful person and character to be loved, admired, and adored. It effectually addresses all the rudimental elements and cravings of our nature, and ministers to them all; as light to the eye, music to the ear, peace to the conscience, and joy to the heart, so it meets and provides for every rational, moral, and religious appetency of our nature in all its conditions and circumstances. It is, indeed, infinitely worthy of God to be the author of it, and of man to be the subject and the object of it.

gracious influential presence from his ordinances, and not unfrequently gives up the contentious authors and abettors of religious discord to fall into grievous scandals, or visits them with judgments, as he did the house of Eli. Thus, while professing Christians bite and devour one another, they are consumed one of another, or fall a prey to the righteous judgments of God; meantime, the truly religious of all parties are grieved, the weak stumbled, the graceless and profane hardened, the mouths of infidels opened to blaspheme religion, and thus the only thing under heaven divinely efficacious to promote and secure the present spiritual and eternal good of man, even the Gospel of the blessed Jesus, is reduced to contempt, while multitudes, deprived of a Gospel ministry, as has been observed, fall an easy prey to seducers, and so become the dupes of almost unheard-of delusions. Are not such the visible effects of our sad divisions, even in this otherwise happy country. Say, dear brethren, are not these things so? Is it not then your incumbent duty to endeavor, by all Scriptural means, to have those evils remedied. Who will say that it is not? And does it not peculiarly belong to *you*, who occupy the place of Gospel ministers, to be leaders in this laudable undertaking? Much depends upon *your* hearty concurrence and zealous endeavors. The favorable opportunity which Divine Providence has put into your hands, in this happy country, for the accomplishment of so great a good, is, in itself, a consideration of no small encouragement. A country happily exempted from the baneful influence of a civil establishment of any peculiar form of Christianity; from under the direct influence of the antichristian hierarchy; and, at the same time, from any formal connection with the devoted nations that have given their strength and power unto the beast; in which, of course, no adequate reformation can be accomplished, until the word of God be fulfilled, and the vials of his wrath poured out upon them. Happy exemption, indeed, from being the object of such awful judgments. Still more happy will it be for us if we duly esteem and improve those great advantages, for the high and valuable ends for which they are manifestly given, and sure where much is given, much also will be required. Can the Lord expect, or require, anything less from a people in such unhampered circumstances — from a people so liberally furnished with all means and mercies, than a thorough reformation in all things, civil and religious, according to his word? Why should we suppose it? And would not such an improvement of our precious privileges be equally conducive to the glory of God, and our own present and everlasting good? The auspicious phenomena of the times furnish collateral arguments of a very encouraging nature, that our dutiful and pious endeavors shall not be in vain in the Lord. Is it not the day of the Lord's vengeance upon the antichristian world — the year of recompenses for the controversy of Zion? Surely, then, the time to favor her is come; even the set time. And is it not said that Zion shall be built in troublous times? Have not greater efforts been made, and more done, for the promulgation of the Gospel among the nations, since the commencement of the French revolution, than had been for many centuries prior to that event? And have not the Churches, both in Europe and America, since that period, discovered a more than usual concern for the removal of contentions, for the healing of divisions, for the restoration of a Christian and brotherly intercourse one with another, and for the promotion of each other's spiritual good, as the printed documents upon those subjects amply testify? Should *we* not, then, be excited by these considerations to concur with all our might, to help forward this good work; that what yet remains to be done, may be fully accomplished. And what though the well-meant endeavors after union have not, in some instances, entirely succeeded to the wish of all parties, should this dissuade us from the attempt! Indeed, should Christians cease to contend earnestly for the sacred articles of faith and duty once delivered to the saints, on account of the opposition and scanty success which, in many instances, attend their faithful and honest endeavors; the Divine cause of truth and righteousness might have long ago been relinquished. And is there anything more formidable in the Goliah schism, than in many other evils which Christians have to combat? Or, has the Captain of Salvation sounded a desist from pursuing, or proclaimed a truce with this deadly enemy that is sheathing its sword in the very bowels of his Church, rending and mangling his mystical body into pieces? Has he said to his servants, Let it alone? If not, where is the warrant for a

cessation of endeavors to have it removed?
On the other hand are we not the better instructed by sage experience, how to proceed in
this business, having before our eyes the
inadvertencies and mistakes of others, which
have hitherto, in many instances, prevented the
desired success? Thus taught by experience,
and happily furnished with the accumulated
instructions of those that have gone before us,
earnestly laboring in this good cause, let us
take unto ourselves the whole armor of God,
and, having our feet shod with the preparation of the Gospel of peace, let us stand fast
by this important duty with all perseverance.
Let none that love the peace of Zion be discouraged, much less offended, because that an
object of such magnitude does not, in the first
instance, come forth recommended by the
express suffrage of the mighty or the many.
This consideration, if duly weighed, will
neither give offense, nor yield discouragement
to any one that considers the nature of the
thing in question in connection with what has
been already suggested. Is it not a matter of
universal right, a duty equally belonging to
every citizen of Zion, to seek her good? In
this respect, no one can claim a preference

above his fellows, as to any peculiar, much less exclusive obligation. And, as for authority, it can have no place in this business; for, surely, none can suppose themselves invested with a Divine right, as to anything peculiarly belonging to them, to call the attention of their brethren to this dutiful and important undertaking. For our part, we entertain no such arrogant presumption; nor are we inclined to impute the thought to any of our brethren, that this good work should be let alone till such time as they may think proper to come forward and sanction the attempt, by their invitation and example. It is an open field, an extensive work, to which all are equally welcome, equally invited.

Should we speak of competency, viewing the greatness of the object, and the manifold difficulties which lie in the way of its accomplishment; we would readily exclaim, with the apostle, Who is sufficient for these things? But, upon recollecting ourselves, neither would *we* be discouraged; persuaded with him, that, as the work in which we are engaged, so, likewise, *our* sufficiency is of God. But, after all, both the mighty and the many are with us. The Lord himself, and all that are truly his people, are declaredly on our side. The prayers of all the Churches, nay, the prayers of Christ himself (John xvii: 20, 23), and of all that have ascended to his heavenly kingdom, are with us. The blessing out of Zion is pronounced upon our undertaking. " Pray for the Peace of Jerusalem; they shall prosper that love thee." With such encouragements as these, what should deter us from the heavenly enterprise, or render hopeless the attempt of accomplishing, in due time, an entire union of all the Churches in faith and practice, according to the word of God? Not that we judge ourselves competent to effect such a thing; we utterly disclaim the thought; but we judge it our bounden duty to make the attempt, by using all due means in our power to promote it; and also, that we have sufficient reason to rest assured that our humble and well-meant endeavors shall not be in vain in the Lord.

The cause that we advocate is not our own peculiar cause, nor the cause of any party, considered as such; it is a common cause, the cause of Christ and our brethren of all denominations. All that we presume, then, is to do what we humbly conceive to be *our* duty, in connection with our brethren; to each of whom it equally belongs, as to us, to exert himself for this blessed purpose. And as we have no just reason to doubt the concurrence of our brethren to accomplish an object so desirable in itself, and fraught with such happy consequences, so neither can we look forward to that happy event which will forever put an end to our hapless divisions, and restore to the Church its primitive unity, purity, and prosperity, but in the pleasing prospect of their hearty and dutiful concurrence.

Dearly beloved brethren, why should *we* deem it a thing incredible that the Church of Christ, in this highly favored country, should resume that original unity, peace, and purity which belong to its constitution, and constitute its glory? Or, is there anything that can be justly deemed necessary for this desirable purpose, both to conform to the model and adopt the practice of the primitive Church, expressly exhibited in the New Testament? Whatever alterations this might produce in any or in all of the Churches, should, we think, neither be deemed inadmissible nor ineligible. Surely such alteration would be every way for the better, and not for the worse, unless we should suppose the divinely inspired rule to be faulty, or defective. Were we, then, in our Church constitution and managements, to exhibit a complete conformity to the apostolic Church, would we not be, in that respect, as perfect as Christ intended we should be? And should not this suffice us?

It is, to us, a pleasing consideration that all the Churches of Christ which mutually acknowledge each other as such, are not only agreed in the great doctrines of faith and holiness, but are also materially agreed as to the positive ordinances of the Gospel institution; so that our differences, at most, are about the things in which the kingdom of God does not consist, that is, about matters of private opinion or human invention. What a pity that the kingdom of God should be divided about such things! Who, then, would not be the first among us to give up human inventions in the worship of God, and to cease from imposing his private opinions upon his brethren, that our breaches might *thus* be healed? Who would not willingly conform to the original pattern laid down in the New Testament, for *this* happy purpose? Our dear brethren of all denominations will please to consider that we have our educational prejudices and particular customs to struggle against as well as they. But this we do sincerely declare, that there is nothing we have hitherto received as matter of faith or practice which is not expressly taught and enjoined in the word of God, either in express terms or approved precedent, that we would not heartily relinquish, that so we might return to the original constitutional unity of the Christian Church; and, in this happy unity, enjoy full communion with all our brethren, in peace and charity. The like dutiful condescension we candidly expect of all that are seriously impressed with a sense of the duty they owe to God, to each other, and to their perishing brethren of mankind. To this we call, we invite, our brethren of all denominations, by all the sacred motives which we have avouched as the impulsive reasons of our thus addressing them.

You are all, dear brethren, equally included as the objects of our love and esteem. With you all we desire to unite in the bonds of an entire Christian unity — Christ alone being the *head,* the center, his word the *rule;* an explicit belief of, and manifest conformity to it, in all things — *the terms.* More than this, you will not require of us; and less we cannot require of you; nor, indeed, can we reasonably suppose any would desire it, for what good purpose would it serve? We dare neither assume nor propose the trite indefinite distinction between essentials and non-essentials, in matters of revealed truth and duty; firmly persuaded, that, whatever may be their comparative importance, simply considered, the high obligation of the Divine authority revealing, or enjoining them, renders the belief or performance of them absolutely essential to us, in so far as we know them. And to be ignorant of anything God has revealed, can neither be our duty nor our privilege. We humbly presume, then, dear brethren, you can have no relevant objection to meet us upon this ground. And, we again beseech you, let it be known that it is the invitation of but few; by your accession we shall be many; and whether few, or many, in the first instance, it is all one with respect to the event which must ultimately await the full information and hearty concurrence of all. Besides, whatever is to be done, must begin, some time, some where; and no matter where, nor by whom, if the Lord puts his hand to the work, it must surely prosper. And has he not been graciously pleased, upon many signal occasions, to bring to pass the greatest events from very small beginnings, and even by means the most unlikely. Duty then is ours; but events belong to God.

We hope, then, what we urge will neither be deemed an unreasonable nor an unseasonable undertaking. Why should it be thought unseasonable? Can any time be assigned, while things continue as they are, that would prove more favorable for such an attempt, or what could be supposed to make it so? Might it be the approximation of parties to a greater nearness, in point of public profession and similarity of customs? Or might it be expected from a gradual decline of bigotry? As to the former, it is a well-known fact, that where the difference is least, the opposition is always managed with a degree of vehemence inversely proportioned to the merits of the cause. With respect to the latter, though we are happy to say, that in some cases and places, and, we hope, universally, bigotry is upon the decline; yet we are not warranted, either by the past or present, to act upon that supposition. We have, as yet, by this means seen no such effect produced; nor indeed could we reasonably expect it; for there will always be multitudes of weak persons in the Church, and these are generally most subject to bigotry; add to this, that while divisions exist, there will always be found interested men who will not fail to support them; nor can we at all suppose that Satan will be idle to improve an advantage so important to the interests of his kingdom. And, let it be further observed upon the whole, that, in matters of similar importance to our secular interests, we would by no means content ourselves with such kind of reasoning. We might further add, that the atttempt here suggested not being of a partial, but of general nature, it can have no just tendency to excite the jealousy, or hurt the feelings of any party. On the contrary, every effort toward a permanent Scriptural unity among the Churches, upon the solid basis of universally acknowledged and self-evident truths, must have the happiest tendency to enlighten and conciliate, by thus manifesting to each other their mutual charity and zeal for the truth: "Whom I love in the truth," saith the apostle, " and not I only, but also all they that have known the truth; for the truth's sake, which is in us, and shall be with us forever." Indeed, if no such Divine and adequate basis of union can be fairly exhibited, as will meet the approbation of every upright and intelligent Christian, nor such mode of procedure adopted in favor of the weak as will not oppress their consciences, then the accomplishment of this grand object upon principle must be forever impossible. There would, upon this supposition, remain no other way of accomplishing it, but merely by voluntary compromise, and good-natured accommodation. That such a thing, however, will be accomplished, one way or other, will not be questioned by any that allow themselves to believe that the commands and prayers of our Lord Jesus Christ will not utterly prove ineffectual. Whatever way, then, it is to be effected, whether upon the solid basis of Divinely revealed truth, or the good-natured principle of Christian forbearance and gracious condescension, is it not equally practicable, equally eligible to us, as ever it can be to any; unless we should suppose ourselves destitute of that Christian temper and discernment which is essentially necessary to qualify us to do the will of our gracious Redeemer, whose express command to his people is, that there be " no

divisions among them; but that they all walk
by the same rule, speak the same thing, and
be perfectly joined together in the same mind,
and in the same judgment?" We believe then
it is as practicable as it is eligible. Let us
attempt it. "Up, and be doing, and the Lord
will be with us."

Are we not all praying for that happy event,
when there shall be but one fold, as there is
but one chief Shepherd? What! shall we pray
for a thing, and not strive to obtain it!! not
use the necessary means to have it accomplished!! What said the Lord to Moses upon
a piece of conduct somewhat similar? "Why
criest thou unto me? Speak unto the children of Israel that they go forward, but lift
thou up thy rod, and stretch out thine hand."
Let the ministers of Jesus but embrace this
exhortation, put their hand to the work, and
encourage the people to go forward upon the
firm ground of obvious truth, to unite in the
bonds of an entire Christian unity; and who
will venture to say that it would not soon be
accomplished? "Cast ye up, cast ye up, prepare the way, take up the stumbling-block out
of the way of my people," saith your God. To
you, therefore, it peculiarly belongs, as the

professed and acknowledged leaders of the people, to go before them in this good work, to remove human opinions and the inventions of men out of the way, by carefully separating this chaff from the pure wheat of primary and authentic revelation; casting out that assumed authority, that enacting and decreeing power by which those things have been imposed and established. To this ministerial department, then, do we look with anxiety. Ministers of Jesus, you can neither be ignorant of nor unaffected with the divisions and corruptions of his Church. His dying commands, his last and ardent prayers for the visible unity of his professing people, will not suffer you to be indifferent in this matter. You will not, you cannot, therefore, be silent upon a subject of such vast importance to his personal glory and the happiness of his people — consistently you cannot; for silence gives consent. You will rather lift up your voice like a trumpet to expose the heinous nature and dreadful consequences of those unnatural and antichristian divisions, which have so rent and ruined the Church of God. Thus, in justice to your station and character, honored of the Lord, would we hopefully anticipate your zealous and faithful efforts to heal the breaches of Zion; that God's dear children might dwell together in unity and love; but if otherwise . . . we forbear to utter it. (See Mal. ii: 1-10.)

O! that ministers and people would but consider that there are no divisions in the grave, nor in that world which lies beyond it! there our divisions must come to an end! we must all unite there! Would to God we could find in our hearts to put an end to our short-lived divisions here; that so we might leave a blessing behind us; even a happy and united Church. What gratification, what utility, in the mean time, can our divisions afford either to ministers or people? Should they be perpetuated till the day of judgment, would they convert one sinner from the error of his ways, or save a soul from death? Have they any tendency to hide the multitude of sins that are so dishonorable to God, and hurtful to his people? Do they not rather irritate and produce them? How innumerable and highly aggravated are the sins they have produced, and are at this day producing, both among professors and profane. We entreat, we beseech you then, dear brethren, by all those considerations, to concur in this blessed and dutiful attempt. What is the work of all, must be done by all. Such was the work of the tabernacle in the wilderness. Such is the work to which you are called, not by the authority of man, but by Jesus Christ, and God the Father, who raised him from the dead. By this authority are you called to raise up the tabernacle of David, that is fallen down among us, and to set it up upon its own base. This you cannot do, while you run every man to his own house, and consult only the interests of his own party. Until you associate, consult, and advise together, and in a friendly and Christian manner explore the subject, nothing can be done. We would therefore, with all due deference and submission, call the attention of our brethren to the obvious and important duty of association. Unite with us in the common cause of simple evangelical Christianity; in this glorious cause we are ready to unite ·with you. United we shall prevail. It is the cause of Christ, and of our brethren throughout all the Churches, of catholic unity, peace, and purity; a cause that must finally prosper in spite of all opposition. Let us unite to promote it. Come forward, then, dear brethren, and help with us. Do not

suffer yourselves to be lulled asleep by that
siren song of the slothful and reluctant professor: "The time is not yet come, the time
is not come, saith he; the time that the Lord's
house should be built." Believe him not. Do
ye not discern the signs of the times? Have
not the two witnesses arisen from their state
of political death, from under the long pro-
scription of ages? Have they not stood upon
their feet, in the presence, and to the con-
sternation and terror of their enemies? Has
not their resurrection been accompanied with
a great earthquake? Has not the tenth part
of the great city been thrown down by it?
Has not this event aroused the nations to
indignation? Have they not been angry, yea,
very angry? Therefore, O Lord, is thy wrath
come upon them, and the time of the dead that
they should be avenged, and that thou
shouldest give reward to thy servants the
prophets, and to them that fear thy name, both
small and great; and that thou shouldest
destroy them that have destroyed the earth.
Who among us has not heard the report of
these things, of these lightnings and thunder-
ings and voices; of this tremendous earthquake and great hail; of these awful convul-

sions and revolutions that have dashed and
are dashing to pieces the nations, like a pot-
ter's vessel? Yea, have not the remote vibra-
tions of this dreadful shock been felt even by
us, whom God has graciously placed at so
great a distance?

What shall we say to these things? Is it
time for us to sit still in our corruptions and
divisions, when the Lord, by his word and
providence, is so loudly and expressly calling
us to repentance, and reformation? "Awake,
awake; put on thy strength, O Zion, put on
thy beautiful garments, O Jerusalem, the holy
city; for henceforth there shall no more come
unto thee the uncircumcised and the unclean.
Shake thyself from the dust, O Jerusalem;
arise, loose thyself from the *bands* of thy neck,
O captive daughter of Zion." Resume that
precious, that dear-bought liberty, wherewith
Christ has made his people free; a liberty
from subjection to any authority but his own,
in matters of religion. Call no man father, no
man master on earth; for one is your master,
even Christ, and all ye are brethren. Stand
fast, therefore, in this precious liberty, and be
not entangled again with the yoke of bondage.
For the vindication of this precious liberty

have we declared ourselves hearty and willing advocates. For this benign and dutiful purpose have we associated, that by so doing we might contribute the mite of our humble endeavors to promote it, and thus invite our brethren to do the same. As the first-fruits of our efforts for this blessed purpose we respectfully present to their consideration the following propositions, relying upon their charity and candor that they will neither despise nor misconstrue our humble and adventurous attempt. If they should in any measure serve, as a preliminary, to open up the way to a permanent Scriptural unity among the friends and lovers of truth and peace throughout the Churches, we shall greatly rejoice at it. We by no means pretend to dictate, and could we propose anything more evident, consistent, and adequate, it should be at their service. Their pious and dutiful attention to an object of such magnitude will induce them to communicate to us their emendations; and thus what is sown in weakness will be raised up in power. For certainly the collective graces that are conferred upon the Church, if duly united and brought to bear upon any point of commanded duty, would be amply sufficient for the right and successful performance of it. "For to one is given by the Spirit the word of wisdom; to another the word of knowledge by the same Spirit; to another faith by the same Spirit; to another the discerning of spirits: but the manifestation of the Spirit is given to every man to profit withal. As every man, therefore, hath received the gift, even so minister the same one to another as good stewards of the manifold grace of God." In the face, then, of such instructions, and with such assurances of an all-sufficiency of Divine grace, as the Church has received from her exalted Head, we can neither justly doubt the concurrence of her genuine members; nor yet their ability, when dutifully acting together, to accomplish anything that is necessary for his glory, and their own good; and certainly their visible unity in truth and holiness, in faith and love, is, of all things, the most conducive to both these, if we may credit the dying commands and prayers of our gracious Lord. In a matter, therefore, of such confessed importance, our Christian brethren, however unhappily distinguished by party names, will not, cannot, withhold their helping hand. We are as heartily willing to be their debtors, as they are indispensably bound to be our benefactors. Come, then, dear brethren, we most humbly beseech you, cause your light to shine upon our weak beginnings, that we may see to work by it. Evince your zeal for the glory of Christ, and the spiritual welfare of your fellow-Christians, by your hearty and zealous co-operation to promote the unity, purity, and prosperity of his Church.

Let none imagine that the subjoined propositions are at all intended as an overture toward a new creed or standard for the Church, or as in any wise designed to be made a term of communion; nothing can be further from our intention. They are merely designed for opening up the way, that we may come fairly and firmly to original ground upon clear and certain premises, and take up things just as the apostles left them; that thus disentangled from the accruing embarrassments of intervening ages, we may stand with evidence upon the same ground on which the Church stood at the beginning. Having said so much to solicit attention and prevent mistake, we submit as follows:

PROP. I. That the Church of Christ upon earth is essentially, intentionally, and constitutionally one; consisting of all those in every place that profess their faith in Christ and obedience to him in all things according to the Scriptures, and that manifest the same by their tempers and conduct, and of none else; as none else can be truly and properly called Christians.

2. That although the Church of Christ upon earth must necessarily exist in particular and distinct societies, locally separate one from another, yet there ought to be no schisms, no uncharitable divisions among them. They ought to receive each other as Christ Jesus hath also received them, to the glory of God. And for this purpose they ought all to walk by the same rule, to mind and speak the same thing; and to be perfectly joined together in the same mind, and in the same judgment.

3. That in order to do this, nothing ought to be inculcated upon Christians as articles of faith; nor required of them as terms of communion, but what is expressly taught and enjoined upon them in the word of God. Nor ought anything to be admitted, as of Divine obligation, in their Church constitution and managements, but what is expressly enjoined by the authority of our Lord Jesus Christ and

his apostles upon the New Testament Church; either in express terms or by approved precedent.

4. That although the Scriptures of the Old and New Testaments are inseparably connected, making together but one perfect and entire revelation of the Divine will, for the edification and salvation of the Church, and therefore in that respect cannot be separated; yet as to what directly and properly belongs to their immediate object, the New Testament is as perfect a constitution for the worship, discipline, and government of the New Testament Church, and as perfect a rule for the particular duties of its members, as the Old Testament was for the worship, discipline, and government of the Old Testament Church, and the particular duties of its members.

5. That with respect to the commands and ordinances of our Lord Jesus Christ, where the Scriptures are silent as to the express time or manner of performance, if any such there be, no human authority has power to interfere, in order to supply the supposed deficiency by making laws for the Church; nor can anything more be required of Christians in such cases, but only that they *so* observe these com-

mands and ordinances as will evidently answer
the declared and obvious end of their institution. Much less has any human authority
power to impose new commands or ordinances
upon the Church, which our Lord Jesus Christ
has not enjoined. Nothing ought to be
received into the faith or worship of the
Church, or be made a term of communion
among Christians, that is not as old as the
New Testament.

6. That although inferences and deductions from Scripture premises, when fairly
inferred, may be truly called the doctrine of
God's holy word, yet are they not formally
binding upon the consciences of Christians
farther than they perceive the connection, and
evidently see that they are so; for their faith
must not stand in the wisdom of men, but in
the power and veracity of God. Therefore,
no such deductions can be made terms of communion, but do properly belong to the after
and progressive edification of the Church.
Hence, it is evident that no such deductions
or inferential truths ought to have any place
in the Church's confession.

7. That although doctrinal exhibitions of
the great system of Divine truths, and defen-

sive testimonies in opposition to prevailing errors, be highly expedient, and the more full and explicit they be for those purposes, the better; yet, as these must be in a great measure the effect of human reasoning, and of course must contain many inferential truths, they ought not to be made terms of Christian communion; unless we suppose, what is contrary to fact, that none have a right to the communion of the Church, but such as possess a very clear and decisive judgment, or are come to a very high degree of doctrinal information; whereas the Church from the beginning did, and ever will, consist of little children and young men, as well as fathers.

8. That as it is not necessary that persons should have a particular knowledge or distinct apprehension of all Divinely revealed truths in order to entitle them to a place in the Church; neither should they, for this purpose, be required to make a profession more extensive than their knowledge; but that, on the contrary, their having a due measure of Scriptural self-knowledge respecting their lost and perishing condition by nature and practice, and of the way of salvation through Jesus Christ, accompanied with a profession of their faith

in and obedience to him, in all things, according to his word, is all that is absolutely necessary to qualify them for admission into his Church.

9. That all that are enabled through grace to make such a profession, and to manifest the reality of it in their tempers and conduct, should consider each other as the precious saints of God, should love each other as brethren, children of the same family and Father, temples of the same Spirit, members of the same body, subjects of the same grace, objects of the same Divine love, bought with the same price, and joint-heirs of the same inheritance. Whom God hath thus joined together no man should dare to put asunder.

10. That division among the Christians is a horrid evil, fraught with many evils. It is antichristian, as it destroys the visible unity of the body of Christ; as if he were divided against himself, excluding and excommunicating a part of himself. It is antiscriptural, as being strictly prohibited by his sovereign authority; a direct violation of his express command. It is antinatural, as it excites Christians to contemn, to hate, and oppose one another, who are bound by the highest and

most endearing obligations to love each other as brethren, even as Christ has loved them. In a word, it is productive of confusion and of every evil work.

11. That (in some instances) a partial neglect of the expressly revealed will of God, and (in others) an assumed authority for making the approbation of human opinions and human inventions a term of communion, by introducing them into the constitution, faith, or worship of the Church, are, and have been, the immediate, obvious, and universally acknowledged causes, of all the corruptions and divisions that ever have taken place in the Church of God.

12. That all that is necessary to the highest state of perfection and purity of the Church upon earth is, first, that none be received as members but such as having that due measure of Scriptural self-knowledge described above, do profess their faith in Christ and obedience to him in all things according to the Scriptures; nor, secondly, that any be retained in her communion longer than they continue to manifest the reality of their profession by their temper and conduct. Thirdly, that her ministers, duly and Scripturally qualified, inculcate

none other things than those very articles of faith and holiness expressly revealed and enjoined in the word of God. Lastly, that in all their administrations they keep close by the observance of all Divine ordinances, after the example of the primitive Church, exhibited in the New Testament; without any additions whatsoever of human opinions or inventions of men.

13. Lastly. That if any circumstantials indispensably necessary to the observance of Divine ordinances be not found upon the page of express revelation, such, and such only, as are absolutely necessary for this purpose should be adopted under the title of human expedients, without any pretense to a more sacred origin, so that any subsequent alteration or difference in the observance of these things might produce no contention nor division in the Church.

From the nature and construction of these propositions, it will evidently appear, that they are laid in a designed subserviency to the declared end of our association; and are exhibited for the express purpose of performing a duty of previous necessity, a duty loudly called for in existing circumstances at the hand of every one that would desire to promote the interests of Zion; a duty not only enjoined, as has been already observed from Isaiah lvii: 14, but which is also there predicted of the faithful remnant as a thing in which they would voluntarily engage. "He that putteth his trust in me shall possess the land, and shall inherit my holy mountain; and shall say, Cast ye up, cast ye up, prepare the way; take up the stumbling-block out of the way of my people." To prepare the way for a permanent Scriptural unity among Christians, by calling up to their consideration fundamental truths, directing their attention to first principles, clearing the way before them by removing the stumbling-blocks — the rubbish of ages, which has been thrown upon it, and fencing it on each side, that in advancing toward the desired object they may not miss the way through mistake or inadvertency, by turning aside to the right hand or to the left, is, at least, the sincere intention of the above propositions. It remains with our brethren now to say, how far they go toward answering this intention. Do they exhibit truths demonstrably evident in the light of Scripture and right reason, so that to deny any part of them the contrary assertion would be manifestly absurd and inadmissible? Considered as a preliminary for the above purpose, are they adequate, so that if acted upon, they would infallibly lead to the desired issue? If evidently defective in either of these respects, let them be corrected and amended, till they become sufficiently evident, adequate, and unexceptionable. In the mean time let them be examined with rigor, with all the rigor that justice, candor, and charity will admit. If we have mistaken the way, we shall be glad to be set right; but if, in the mean time, we have been happily led to suggest obvious and undeniable truths, which, if adopted and acted upon, would infallibly lead to the desired unity, and secure it when obtained, we hope it will be no objection that they have not proceeded from a General Council. It is not the voice of the multitude, but the voice of truth, that has power with the conscience; that can produce rational conviction and acceptable obedience. A conscience that awaits the decision of the multitude, that hangs in suspense for the casting vote of the majority, is a fit subject for the man of sin. This, we are persuaded, is the uniform sentiment of real Christians of every denomination. Would to God that all professors were such, then should our eyes soon behold the prosperity of Zion; we should soon see Jerusalem a quiet habitation. Union in truth has been, and ever must be, the desire and prayer of all such; "Union in Truth" is our motto. The Divine word is our standard; in the Lord's name do we display our banners. Our eyes are upon the promises, "So shall they fear the name of the Lord from the west, and his glory from the rising of the sun." "When the enemy shall come in like a flood the Spirit of the Lord shall lift up a standard against him." Our humble desire is to be his standard-bearers, to fight under *his* banner, and with *his* weapons, "which are not carnal, but mighty through God to the pulling down of strongholds;" even all these strongholds of division, those partition walls of separation, which, like the walls of Jericho, have been built up, as it were, to the very heavens, to separate God's people, to divide *his* flock and so to prevent them from entering into their promised rest, at least in so far as it respects this world. An enemy hath done this, but he shall not finally prevail; "for the meek shall inherit the earth, and shall delight themselves in the abundance of peace."

"And the kingdom and dominion, even the greatness of the kingdom under the whole heaven, shall be given to the people of the saints of the Most High, and they shall possess it forever." But this can not be in their present broken and divided state; "for a kingdom or a house divided against itself cannot stand; but cometh to desolation." Now this has been the case with the Church for a long time. However, "the Lord will not cast off his people, neither will he forsake his heritage; but judgment shall return unto righteousness, and all the upright in heart shall follow it." To all such, and such alone, are our expectations directed. Come, then, ye blessed of the Lord, we have your prayers, let us also have your actual assistance. What, shall we pray for a thing and not strive to obtain it!

We call, we invite you again, by every consideration in these premises. You that are near, associate with us; you that are at too great a distance, associate as we have done. Let not the paucity of your number in any given district, prove an insuperable discouragement. Remember Him that has said, "If two of you shall agree on earth as touching anything that they shall ask, it shall be done for

them of my Father who is in heaven: for
where two or three are gathered together in
my name, there am I in the midst of them."
With such a promise as this, for the attainment
of every possible and promised good, there is
no room for discouragement. Come on then,
" ye that fear the Lord; keep not silence, and
give him no rest till he make Jerusalem a joy
and a praise in the earth." Put on that noble
resolution dictated by the prophet, saying,
" For Zion's sake will we not hold our peace,
and for Jerusalem's sake we will not rest, until
the righteousness thereof go forth as bright-
ness, and the salvation thereof as a lamp that
burneth." Thus impressed, you will find
means to associate at such convenient distances, as to meet at least once a month; to
beseech the Lord to put an end to our lamentable divisions; to heal and unite his people,
that his Church may resume her original constitutional unity and purity, and thus be
exalted to the enjoyment of her promised prosperity, that the Jews may be speedily converted, and the fullness of the Gentiles brought
in. Thus associated, you will be in a capacity to investigate the evil causes of our sad
divisions; to consider and bewail their perni-

cious effects; and to mourn over them before the Lord — who hath said: " I will go and return to my place, till they acknowledge their offense and seek my face." Alas! then, what reasonable prospect can we have of being delivered from those sad calamities, which have so long afflicted the Church of God; while a party spirit, instead of bewailing, is everywhere justifying, the bitter principle of these pernicious evils; by insisting upon the right of rejecting those, however unexceptionable in other respects, who cannot see with them in matters of private opinion, of human inference, that are nowhere expressly revealed or enjoined in the word of God. Thus associated, will the friends of peace, the advocates for Christian unity, be in a capacity to connect in larger circles, where several of those smaller societies may meet semi-annually at a convenient center; and thus avail themselves of their combined exertions for promoting the interests of the common cause. We hope that many of the Lord's ministers in all places will volunteer in this service, forasmuch as they know it is his favorite work, the very desire of his soul.

You lovers of Jesus, and beloved of him,

however scattered in this cloudy and dark day, you love the truth as it is in Jesus; (if our hearts deceive us not) so do we. You desire union in Christ with all them that love him; so do we. You lament and bewail our sad divisions; so do we. You reject the doctrines and commandments of men, that you may keep the law of Christ; so do we. You believe that the word itself ought to be our rule, and not any human explication of it; so do we. You believe that no man has a right to judge, to exclude, or reject his professing Christian brother, except in so far as he stands condemned or rejected by the express letter of the law; so do we. You believe that the great fundamental law of unity and love ought not to be violated to make way for exalting human opinions to an equality with express revelation, by making them articles of faith and terms of communion; so do we. You sincere and impartial followers of Jesus, friends of truth and peace, we dare not, we cannot think otherwise of you; it would be doing violence to your character; it would be inconsistent with your prayers and profession so to do. We shall therefore have *your* hearty concurrence. But if any of our dear brethren, from whom we should expect better things, should, through weakness or prejudice, be in anything otherwise minded than we have ventured to suppose, we charitably hope that, in due time, God will reveal even this unto them; only let such neither refuse to come to the light, nor yet, through prejudice, reject it when it shines upon them. Let them rather seriously consider what we have thus most seriously and respectfully submitted to their consideration; weigh every sentiment in the balance of the sanctuary, as in the sight of God, with earnest prayer for, and humble reliance upon, his Spirit, and not in the spirit of self-sufficiency and party zeal; and, in so doing, we rest assured, the consequence will be happy, both for their own and the Church's peace. Let none imagine, that in so saying, we arrogate to ourselves a degree of intelligence superior to our brethren; much less superior to mistake. So far from this, our confidence is entirely founded upon the express Scripture and matter-of-fact evidence of the things referred to; which may, nevertheless, through inattention or prejudice, fail to produce their proper effect, as has been the case with respect to some of the most evident truths in a thou-

sand instances. But charity thinketh no evil;
and we are far from surmising, though we
must speak. To warn, even against possible
evils, is certainly no breach of charity, as to
be confident of the certainty of some things
is no just argument of presumption. We by
no means claim the approbation of our
brethren as to anything we have suggested for
promoting the sacred cause of Christian unity,
further than it carries its own evidence along
with it; but we humbly claim a fair investigation of the subject, and solicit the assistance of
our brethren for carrying into effect what we
have thus weakly attempted. It is our consola-
tion, in the mean time, that the desired event,
as certain as it will be happy and glorious,
admits of no dispute, however we may hesitate
or differ about the proper means of promoting
it. All we shall venture to say as to this is,
that we trust we have taken the proper ground;
at least, if we have not, we despair of finding
it elsewhere. For, if holding fast in profession
and practice whatever is expressly revealed and
enjoined in the Divine standard does not,
under the promised influence of the Divine
Spirit, prove an adequate basis for promoting
and maintaining unity, peace, and purity, we

utterly despair of attaining those invaluable privileges, by adopting the standard of any party. To advocate the cause of unity, while espousing the interests of a party, would appear as absurd as for this country to take part with either of the belligerents in the present awful struggle, which has convulsed and is convulsing, the nations, in order to maintain her neutrality and secure her peace. Nay, it would be adopting the very means by which the bewildered Church has, for hundreds of years past, been rending and dividing herself into factions, for Christ's sake, and for the truth's sake; though the first and foundation truth of our Christianity is union with him, and the very next to it in order, union with each other in him —"that we receive each other, as Christ has also received us, to the glory of God." "For this is his commandment: That we believe in his Son Jesus Christ, and love one another, as he gave us commandment. And he that keepeth his commandments dwelleth in him, and he in him; and hereby we know that he dwelleth in us, by the Spirit which he hath given us," even the spirit of faith, and of love, and of a sound mind. And surely this should suffice us. But how to love and receive our brother, as we believe and hope Christ has received both him and us, and yet refuse to hold communion with him, is, we confess, a mystery too deep for us. If this be the way that Christ hath received us, then woe is unto us. We do not here intend a professed brother transgressing the express letter of the law, and refusing to be reclaimed. Whatever may be our charity in such a case, we have not sufficient evidence that Christ has received him, or that he has received Christ as his teacher and Lord. To adopt means, then, apparently subversive of the very end proposed, means which the experience of ages has evinced successful only in overthrowing the visible interests of Christianity, in counteracting, as far as possible, the declared intention, the express command of its Divine author, would appear in no wise a prudent measure for removing and preventing those evils. To maintain unity and purity has always been the plausible pretense of the compilers and abettors of human systems, and we believe, in many instances, their sincere intention; but have they at all answered the end? Confessedly, demonstrably, they have not; no, not even in the several parties which have most strictly adopted them; much less to the catholic professing body. Instead of her catholic constitutional unity and purity, what does the Church present us with, at this day, but a catalogue of sects and sectarian systems — each binding its respective party, by the most sacred and solemn engagements, to continue as it is to the end of the world; at least, this is confessedly the case with many of them. What a sorry substitute these for Christian unity and love! On the other hand, what a mercy is it that no human obligation that man can come under is valid against the truth. When the Lord the healer descends upon his people, to give them a discovery of the nature and tendency of those artificial bonds wherewith they have suffered themselves to be bound in their dark and sleepy condition, they will no more be able to hold them in a state of sectarian bondage than the withes and cords with which the Philistines bound Samson were able to retain him their prisoner, or than the bonds of Antichrist were to hold in captivity the fathers of the Reformation. May

the Lord soon open the eyes of his people to
see things in their true light, and excite them
to come up out of their wilderness condition,
out of this Babel of confusion, leaning upon
their Beloved, and embracing each other in
him, holding fast the unity of the spirit in the
bond of peace. This gracious unity and
unanimity in Jesus would afford the best external evidence of their union with him, and of
their conjoint interest in the Father's love.
" By this shall all men know that you are my
disciples," says he, " if you have love one to
another." And " This is my commandment,
That you love one another as I have loved you ;
that you also love one another." And again,
" Holy Father, keep through thine own name
those whom thou hast given me, that they may
be one, as we are ;" even " all that shall believe
in me; that they all may be one; as thou,
Father, art in me and I in thee, that they also
may be one in us : that the world may believe
that thou hast sent me. And the glory which
thou gavest me, I have given them; that they
may be one, even as we are one; I in them,
and thou in me, that they may be made perfect
in one; and that the world may know that

thou hast sent me, and hast loved them as thou hast loved me." May the Lord hasten it in his time. Farewell.

Peace be with all them that love our Lord Jesus Christ in sincerity. Amen.

THOMAS CAMPBELL,
THOMAS ACHESON.

APPENDIX.

To prevent mistakes, we beg leave to subjoin the following explanations. As to what we have done, our reasons for so doing, and the grand object we would desire to see accomplished, all these, we presume, are sufficiently declared in the foregoing pages. As to what we intend to do in our associate capacity, and the ground we have taken in that capacity, though expressly and definitely declared, yet these, perhaps, might be liable to some misconstruction. First, then, we beg leave to assure our brethren that we have no intention to interfere, either directly or indirectly, with the peace and order of the settled Churches, by directing any ministerial assistance with which the Lord may please to favor us, to make inroads upon such; or by endeavoring to erect Churches out of Churches, to distract and divide congregations. We have no nostrum, no peculiar discovery of our own to propose to fellow-Christians, for the fancied importance of which they should become followers of us. We propose to patronize nothing but the inculcation of the express word of God, either as to matter of faith or practice; but every one that has a Bible, and can read it, can read this for himself. Therefore, we have nothing new. Neither do we pretend to acknowledge persons to be ministers of Christ, and, at the same time, consider it our duty to forbid or discourage people to go to hear them, merely because they may hold some things disagreeable to us; much less to encourage their people to leave them on that account. And such do we esteem all who preach a free, unconditional* salvation through the blood of

---

* *"Unconditional"* salvation. There is neither *conditional* nor *unconditional* salvation so designated in holy Scripture. As respects procurement, there is no condition. *It is of grace.* But, like *life* and *health,* there are conditions of enjoyment. We could not procure, merit, or purchase it at any price. But when justified by faith and not by works, sanctified by the Spirit, or separated from the world, we are commanded to give "all diligence to make our calling and election sure."

There are means of spiritual life and health, as well as means of temporal or animal life and health. The latter are not more necessary than the former. God's

Jesus to perishing sinners of every description, and who manifestly connect with this a life of holiness and pastoral diligence in the performance of all the duties of their sacred office, according to the Scriptures, of even all of whom, as to all appearance, it may be truly said to the objects of their charge: " They seek not *yours,* but *you.*" May the good Lord prosper all such, by whatever name they are called, and hasten that happy period when Zion's watchmen shall see eye to eye, and all be called by the same name. *Such,* then, have nothing to fear from our association, were our resources equal to our utmost wishes. But all others we esteem as hirelings, as idle shepherds, and should be glad to see the Lord's flock delivered from their mouth, according

whole universe is one great system of means and ends — physical, intellectual, moral, and religious. The means and the ends are alike of Divine institution, and are, therefore, inseparable.

The word *means* is found in the common version of the Christian Scriptures only *twenty-one times.* Two-thirds of these are found in Paul's writings. *Poos* or *cipoos* — "how," or *by what means* — are equivalent terms. The *how* case and the *why* case are quite dissimilar. The *why* case demands the *cause.* The *how* case demands the *means.* Our English dictionaries authenticate these distinctions. They are, however, frequently unheeded in the pulpit and in the press.

to his promise. Our principal and proper
design, then, with respect to ministerial assist-
ants, such as we have described in our fifth
resolution, is to direct their attention to those
places where there is manifest need for their
labors; and many such places there are;
would to God it were in our power to supply
them. As to creeds and confessions, although
we may appear to our brethren to oppose them,
yet this is to be understood only in *so far* as
they oppose the unity of the Church, by containing sentiments not expressly revealed in
the word of God; or, by the way of using
them, become the instruments of a human or
implicit faith, or oppress the weak of God's
heritage. Where they are liable to none of
those objections, we have nothing against
them. It is the *abuse* and not the *lawful use*
of such compilations that we oppose. See
Proposition 7, page 50. Our intention, therefore, with respect to all the Churches of Christ
is perfectly amicable. We heartily wish their
reformation, but by no means their hurt or
confusion. Should any affect to say that our
coming forward as we have done, in advancing and publishing such things, has a manifest tendency to distract and divide the

Churches, or to make a new party, we treat it as a confident and groundless assertion, and must suppose they have not duly considered, or, at least, not well understood the subject.

All we shall say to this at present, is, that if the Divine word be not the standard of a party, then are we not a party, for we have adopted no other. If to maintain its alone sufficiency be not a party principle, then are we not a party. If to justify this principle by our practice, in making a rule of it, and of *it alone,* and not of our own opinions, nor of those of others, be not a party principle, then are we not a party. If to propose and practice neither more nor less than it expressly reveals and enjoins be not a partial business, then are we not a party. These are the very sentiments we have approved and recommended, as a society formed for the express purpose of promoting Christian unity, in opposition to a party spirit. Should any tell us that to do these things is impossible without the intervention of human reason and opinion, we humbly thank them for the discovery. But who ever thought otherwise? Were we not rational subjects, and of course capable of understanding and forming opinions, would it not evidently appear that, to us, revelation of any kind would be quite useless, even suppose it as evident as mathematics? We pretend not, therefore, to divest ourselves of reason, that me may become quiet, inoffensive, and peaceable Christians; nor yet, of any of its proper and legitimate operations upon Divinely revealed truths. We only pretend to assert, what every one that pretends to reason must acknowledge, namely, that there is a manifest distinction between an express Scripture declaration, and the conclusion or inference which may be deduced from it; and that the former may be clearly understood, even where the latter is but imperfectly if at all perceived; and that we are at least as certain of the declaration as we can be of the conclusion we drew from it; and that, after all, the conclusion ought not to be exalted above the premises, so as to make void the declaration for the sake of establishing our own conclusion; and that, therefore, the express commands to preserve and maintain inviolate Christian unity and love, ought not to be set aside to make way for exalting our inferences above the express authority of God. Our inference, upon the whole, is, that where a professing Christian brother opposes or refuses nothing either in faith or practice, for which there can be expressly produced a " Thus saith the Lord," that we ought not to reject him because he cannot see with our eyes as to matters of human inference, of private judgment. " Through thy knowledge shall the weak brother perish? How walkest thou not charitably?" Thus we reason, thus we conclude, to make no conclusion of our own, nor of any other fallible fellow-creature, a rule of faith or duty to our brother. Whether we refuse reason, then, or abuse it, in our so doing, let our brethren judge. But, after all, we have only ventured to suggest what, in other words, the apostle has expressly taught; namely, that the strong ought to bear with the infirmities of the weak, and not to please themselves; that we ought to receive him that is weak in the faith, because God has received him. In a word, that we ought to receive one another, as Christ hath also received us to the glory of God. We dare not, therefore, patronize the rejection of God's dear children, because they may not be able to see alike in matters of human inference — of private opinion; and such we esteem all things not expressly revealed and enjoined

in the word of God. If otherwise, we know
not what private opinion means. On the other
hand, should our peaceful and affectionate
overture for union in truth prove offensive to
any of our brethren, or occasion disturbances
in any of the Churches, the blame cannot be
attached to us. We have only ventured to
persuade, and, if possible, to excite to the performance of an important duty — a duty
equally incumbent upon us all. Neither have
we pretended to dictate to *them* what *they*
should do. We have only proposed what
appeared to us most likely to promote the
desired event, humbly submitting the whole
premises to their candid and impartial investigation, to be altered, corrected, and amended,
as they see cause, or to adopt any other plan
that may appear more just and unexceptionable. As for ourselves, we have taken all due
care, in the mean time, to take no step that
might throw a stumbling-block in the way,
that might prove now, or at any future period,
a barrier to prevent the accomplishment of
that most desirable object, either by joining
to support a party, or by patronizing anything
as articles of faith or duty not expressly enjoined in the Divine standard; as we are sure,

whatever alterations may take place, *that* will stand. That considerable alterations must and will take place, in the standards of all the sects, before that glorious object can be accomplished, no man, that duly considers the matter, can possibly doubt. In so far, then, we have at least endeavored to act consistently; and with the same consistency would desire to be instrumental in erecting as many Churches as possible throughout the desolate places of God's heritage, upon the same catholic foundation, being well persuaded that every such erection will not only in the issue prove an accession to the general cause, but will also, in the mean time, be a step toward it, and, of course, will reap the first-fruits of that blissful harvest that will fill the face of the world with fruit. For if the first Christian Churches, walking in the fear of the Lord in holy unity and unanimity, enjoyed the comforts of the Holy Spirit, and were increased and edified, we have reason to believe that walking in their footsteps will everywhere and at all times insure the same blessed privileges. And it is in an exact conformity to their recorded and approved example, that we, through grace, would be desirous to promote the erection of

Churches; and this we believe to be quite practicable, if the legible and authentic records of *their* faith and practice be handed down to *us* upon the page of New Testament Scripture; but if otherwise, we cannot help it. Yet, even in this case, might we not humbly presume that the Lord would take the will for the deed? for if there be first a willing mind, we are told, " it is accepted according to what a man hath, and not according to what he hath not." It would appear, then, that sincerely and humbly adopting this model, with an entire reliance upon promised grace, we cannot, we shall not, be disappointed. By this, at least, we shall get rid of two great evils, which, we fear, are at this day grievously provoking the Lord to plead a controversy with the Churches: we mean the taking and giving of unjust offenses; judging and rejecting each other in matters wherein the Lord hath not judged, in a flat contradiction to his expressly revealed will. But, according to the principle adopted, we can neither take offense at our brother for his private opinions, if he be content to hold them as such, nor yet offend him with ours, if he do not usurp the place of the lawgiver; and even suppose he should, in this case we judge him, not for his *opinions,* but for his *presumption.* "There is one Lawgiver, who is able to save and to destroy: who art thou that judgest another?" But further, to prevent mistakes, we beg leave to explain our meaning in a sentence or two which might possibly be misunderstood. In the first page we say, that no man has a right to judge his brother, except in so far as he manifestly violates the express letter of the law. By the law here, and elsewhere, when taken in this latitude, we mean that whole revelation of faith and duty expressly declared in the Divine word, taken together, or in its due connection, upon every article, and not any detached sentence. We understand it as extending to all prohibitions, as well as to all requirements. "Add thou not unto his words, lest he reprove thee, and thou be found a liar." We dare, therefore, neither do nor receive anything as of Divine obligation for which there cannot be expressly produced a "Thus saith the Lord," either in express terms or by approved precedent. According to this rule we judge, and beyond it we dare not go. Taking this sentiment in connection with the last clause of the fifth resolution, we are to be understood, of all matters of faith and practice, of primary and universal obligation; that is to say, of express revelation; that nothing be inculcated, as such, for which there cannot be expressly produced a "Thus saith the Lord," as above, without, at the same time, interfering directly or indirectly with the private judgment of any individual, which does not expressly contradict the express letter of the law, or add to the number of its institutions. Every sincere and upright Christian will understand and do the will of God, in every instance, to the best of his skill and judgment; but in the application of the general rule to particular cases there may, and doubtless will, be some variety of opinion and practice. This, we see, was actually the case in the apostolic Churches, without any breach of Christian unity; and if this was the case at the erection of the Christian Church from among Jews and Gentiles, may we not reasonably expect that it will be the same at her restoration from under her long antichristian and sectarian desolations?

With a direct reference to this state of things, and, as we humbly think, in a perfect consistency with the foregoing explanations, have we expressed ourselves in the thirty-ninth page, wherein we declare ourselves ready to relinquish whatever we have hitherto received as matter of faith or practice, not expressly taught and enjoined in the word of God, so that we and our brethren might, by this mutual concession, return together to the original constitutional unity of the Christian Church, and dwell together in peace and charity. By this proposed relinquishment we are to be understood, in the first instance, of our manner of holding those things, and not simply of the things themselves; for no man can relinquish his opinions or practices till once convinced that they are wrong; and this he may not be immediately, even supposing they were so. One thing, however, he may do: when not bound by an express command, he need not impose them upon others, by anywise requiring their approbation; and when this is done, the things, to them, are as good as dead, yea, as good as buried, too, being thus removed out of the way. Has not the apostle set us a noble example of this in his pious and charitable zeal for the comfort and edification of his brother, in declaring himself ready to forego his rights (not indeed to break commandments) rather than stumble, or offend, his brother? And who knows not that the Hebrew Christians abstained from certain meats, observed certain days, kept the passover, circumcised their children, etc., etc., while no such things were practiced by the Gentile converts, and yet no breach of unity while they charitably forbore one with the other. But had the Jews been expressly prohibited, or the Gentiles expressly enjoined, by the authority of Jesus, to observe these things, could they, in such a case, have lawfully exercised this forbearance? But where no express law is, there can be no formal, no intentional transgression, even although its implicit and necessary consequences had forbid the thing, had they been discovered. Upon the whole, we see one thing is evident: the Lord will bear with the weaknesses, the involuntary ignorances, and mistakes of his people, though not with their presumption. Ought they not, therefore, to bear with each other —" to preserve the unity of the Spirit in the bond of peace; forbearing one with another in love? " What says the Scripture? We say, then, the declaration referred to is to be thus understood in the first instance; though we do not say but something further is intended. For certainly we may lawfully suspend both declaration and practice upon any subject, where the law is silent; when to do otherwise must prevent the accomplishment of an expressly commanded and highly important duty; and such, confessedly, is the thing in question. What says the apostle? "All things are lawful for me; but all things are not expedient. All things are lawful for me; but all things edify not." It seems, then, that among lawful things which might be forborne — that is, as we humbly conceive, things not expressly commanded — the governing principle of the apostle's conduct was the edification of his brethren of the Church of God. A Divine principle this, indeed! May the Lord God infuse it into all his people. Were all those nonpreceptive opinions and practices which have been maintained and exalted to the destruction of the Church's unity, counterbalanced with the breach of the express law of Christ, and the black catalogue of mischiefs which have necessarily ensued, on which side, think you, would be the preponderance? When weighed in the balance with this monstrous complex evil, would they not all appear lighter than vanity?

Who, then, would not relinquish a cent to obtain a kingdom! And here let it be noted, that it is not the renunciation of an opinion or practice as sinful that is proposed or intended, but merely a cessation from the publishing or practicing it, so as to give offense; a thing men are in the habit of doing every day for their private comfort or secular emolument, where the advantage is of infinitely less importance. Neither is there here any clashing of duties, as if to forbear was a sin and also to practice was sin; the thing to be forborne being a matter of private opinion, which, though not expressly forbidden, yet are we by no means expressly commanded to practice; whereas we are expressly commanded to endeavor to maintain the unity of the Spirit in the bond of peace. And what says the apostle to the point in hand? "Hast thou faith," says he; "have it to thyself before God. Happy is the man that condemneth not himself in the thing which he alloweth."

It may be further added, that a still higher and more perfect degree of uniformity is intended, though neither in the first nor second instance, which are but so many steps toward it; namely: the utter abolition of those minor differences, which have been greatly increased, as well as continued, by our unhappy manner of treating them, in making them the subject of perpetual strife and contention. Many of the opinions which are now dividing the Church, had they been let alone, would have been long since dead and gone; but the constant insisting upon them, as articles of faith and terms of salvation, have so beaten them into the minds of men, that, in many instances, they would as soon deny the Bible itself as give up one of those opinions. Having thus embraced contentions and preferred divisions to that constitutional unity, peace, and charity so essential to Christianity, it would appear that the Lord, in righteous judgment, has abandoned his professing people to the awful scourge of those evils; as, in an instance somewhat similar, he formerly did his highly favored Israel. " My people," says he, " would not hearken to my voice. So I gave them up to their own hearts' lusts, and they walked in their own counsels." " Israel hath made many altars to sin: therefore altars shall be unto him to sin." Thus, then, are we to be consistently understood, as fully and fairly intending, on *our* part, what we have declared and proposed to our brethren, as, to *our* apprehension, incumbent upon *them* and *us,* for putting an end forever to our sad and lamentable schisms. Should any object and say that, after all, the fullest compliance with everything proposed and intended would not restore the Church to the desired unity, as there might remain differences of opinion and practice; let such but duly consider what properly belongs to the unity of the Church, and we are persuaded this objection will vanish. Does not the visible Scriptural unity of the Christian Church consist in the unity of her public profession and practice, and, under this, in the manifest charity of her members, one toward another, and not in the unity of private opinion and practice of every individual? Was not this evidently the case in the apostles' days, as has been already observed? If so, the objection falls to the ground. And here let it be noted (if the hint be at all necessary), that we are speaking of the unity of the Church considered as a great, visible, professing body, consisting of many co-ordinate associations; each of these, in its aggregate or associate capacity, walking by the same rule, professing and practicing the same things. That this visible

Scriptural unity be preserved without corruption, or breach of charity, throughout the whole, and in every particular worshiping society or Church, is the grand desideratum — the thing strictly enjoined and greatly to be desired. An agreement in the expressly revealed will of God is the adequate and firm foundation of this unity; ardent prayer, accompanied with prudent, peaceable, and persevering exertion, in the use of all Scriptural means for accomplishing it, are the things humbly suggested and earnestly recommended to our brethren. If we have mistaken the way, their charity will put us right; but if otherwise, their fidelity to Christ and his cause will excite them to come forth speedily, to assist with us in this blessed work.

After all, should any impeach us with the vague charge of Latitudinarianism (let none be startled at this gigantic term), it will prove as feeble an opponent to the glorious cause in which we, however weak and unworthy, are professedly engaged, as the Zamzummins did of old, to prevent the children of Lot from taking possession of their inheritance. If we take no greater latitude than the Divine law allows, either in judging of persons or doctrines — either in profession or practice (and this is the very thing we humbly propose and sincerely intend), may we not reasonably hope that such a latitude will appear, to every upright Christian, perfectly innocent and unexceptionable? If this be Latitudinarianism, it must be a good thing, and, therefore, the more we have of it the better; and may be it is, for we are told, "the commandment is exceeding broad;" and we intend to go just as far as it will suffer us, but not one hairbreadth further; so, at least, says our profession. And surely it will be time enough to condemn our practice, when it appears manifestly inconsistent with the profession we have thus precisely and explicitly made. We here refer to the whole of the foregoing premises. But were this word as bad as it is long, were it stuffed with evil from beginning to end, may be it better belongs to those that brandish it so unmercifully at their neighbors, especially if they take a greater latitude than their neighbors do, or than the Divine law allows. Let the case, then, be fairly submitted to all that know their Bible, to all that take upon them to see with their own eyes, to judge for themselves. And here let it be observed once for all, that it is only to such we direct our attention in the foregoing pages. As for those that either cannot or will not see and judge for themselves, they must be content to follow their leaders till they come to their eyesight, or determine to make use of the faculties and means of information which God has given them; with such, in the mean time, it would be useless to reason, seeing that they either confessedly cannot see, or have completely resigned themselves to the conduct of their leaders, and are therefore determined to hearken to none but them. If there be none such, however, we are happily deceived; but, if so, we are not the only persons that are thus deceived; for this is the common fault objected by almost all the parties to each other, namely, that they either cannot or will not see; and it would be hard to think they were all mistaken; the fewer there be, however, of this description, the better. To all those, then, that are disposed to see and think for themselves, to form their judgment by the Divine word itself, and not by any human explication of it, humbly relying upon and looking for the promised assistance of Divine teaching, and not barely trusting to their own understanding — to all such do we gladly commit our cause, being persuaded that, at least, they will give it a very serious and impartial consideration, as being truly desirous to know the truth. To you, then, we appeal, in the present instance, as we have also done from the beginning. Say, we beseech you, to whom does the charge of Latitudinarianism, when taken in a bad sense (for we have supposed it may be taken in a good sense), most truly and properly belong, whether to those that will neither add nor diminish anything as to matter of faith and duty, either to or from what is expressly revealed and enjoined in the holy Scriptures, or to those who pretend to go further than this, or to set aside some of its express declarations and injunctions, to make way for their own opinions, inferences, and conclusions? Whether to those who profess their willingness to hold communion with their acknowledged Christian brethren, when they neither manifestly oppose nor contradict anything expressly revealed and enjoined in the sacred standard, or to those who reject such, when professing to believe and practice whatever is expressly revealed and enjoined therein, without, at the same time, being *alleged,* much less *found* guilty, of anything to the contrary, but instead of this asserting and declaring their hearty assent and consent to everything for which there can be expressly produced a " Thus saith the Lord," either in express terms or by approved precedent? To which of these, think you, does the odious charge of Latitudinarianism belong? Which of them takes the greatest latitude? Whether those that expressly judge and condemn where they have no express warrant for so doing, or those that absolutely refuse so to do? And we can assure our brethren, that such things are and have been done, to our own certain knowledge, and even where we least expected it; and that it is to this discovery, as much as to many other things, that we stand indebted for that thorough conviction of the evil state of things in the Churches, which has given rise to our association. As for our part, we dare no longer give our assent to such proceedings; we dare no longer concur in expressly asserting or declaring anything in the name of the Lord, that he has not expressly declared in his holy word. And until such time as Christians come to see the evil of doing otherwise, we see no rational ground to hope that there can be either unity, peace, purity, or prosperity, in the Church of God. Convinced of the truth of this, we would humbly desire to be instrumental in pointing out to our fellow-Christians the evils of such conduct. And if we might venture to give our opinion of such proceedings, we would not hesitate to say, that they appear to include three great evils — evils truly great in themselves, and at the same time productive of most evil consequences.

First, to determine expressly, in the name of the Lord, when the Lord has not expressly determined, appears to us a very great evil. (See Deut. xviii: 20:) "The prophet that shall presume to speak a word in my name, which I have not commanded him to speak, even that prophet shall die." The apostle Paul, no doubt, well aware of this, cautiously distinguishes between his own judgment and the express injunctions of the Lord. (See 1 Cor. vii: 25 and 40.) Though, at the same time, it appears that he was as well convinced of the truth and propriety of his declarations, and of the concurrence of the Holy Spirit with his judgment, as any of our modern determiners may be; for "I think," said he, "that I have the Spirit of God;" and we doubt much, if the best of them could honestly say more than this; yet we see that, with all this, he would not bind the Church with his conclusions; and, for this very reason, as he expressly tells us, because, as to the matter on hand, he had no commandment of the Lord. He spoke by permission, and not by commandment, as one that had obtained mercy to be faithful, and therefore would not forge his Master's name by affixing it to his own conclusions, saying, "The Lord saith, when the Lord had not spoken."

A second evil is, not only judging our brother to be absolutely wrong, because he differs from our opinions, but more especially, our judging him to be a transgressor of the law in so doing, and, of course, treating him as such by censuring or otherwise exposing him to contempt, or, at least, preferring ourselves before him in our own judgment, saying, as it were, Stand by, I am holier than thou.

A third and still more dreadful evil is, when we not only, in this kind of way, judge and set at naught our brother, but, moreover, proceed as a Church, acting and judging in the name of Christ, not only to determine that our brother is wrong because he differs from our

determinations, but also, in connection with
this, proceed so far as to determine the merits
of the cause by rejecting him, or casting him
out of the Church, as unworthy of a place in
her communion, and thus, as far as in our
power, cutting him off from the kingdom of
heaven. In proceeding thus, we not only
declare, that, in our judgment, our brother is
in an error, which we may sometimes do in a
perfect consistence with charity, but we also
take upon us to judge, as acting in the name
and by the authority of Christ, that his error
cuts him off from salvation; that continuing
such, he has no inheritance in the kingdom of
Christ and of God. If not, what means our
refusing him — our casting him out of the
Church, which is the kingdom of God in this
world? For certainly, if a person have no
right, according to the Divine word, to a place
in the Church of God upon earth (which we
say he has not, by thus rejecting him), he can
have none to a place in the Church in heaven
— unless we should suppose that those whom
Christ by his word rejects here, he will nevertheless receive hereafter. And surely it is by
the word that every Church pretends to judge;
and it is by this rule, in the case before us,

that the person in the judgment of the Church stands rejected. Now is not this, to all intents and purposes, determining the merits of the cause? Do we not conclude that the person's error cuts him off from all ordinary possibility of salvation, by thus cutting him off from a place in the Church, out of which there is no ordinary possibility of salvation? Does he not henceforth become to us as a heathen man and a publican? Is he not reckoned among the number of those that are without, whom God judgeth? If not, what means such a solemn determination? Is it anything or is it nothing, for a person to stand rejected by the Church of God? If such rejection confessedly leave the man still in the same safe and hopeful state as to his spiritual interests, then, indeed, it becomes a matter of mere indifference; for as to his civil and natural privileges, it interferes not with them. But the Scripture gives us a very different view of the matter; for there we see that those that stand justly rejected by the Church on earth, have no room to hope for a place in the Church of heaven. "What ye bind on earth shall be bound in heaven" is the awful sanction of the Church's judgment, in justly rejecting any person.

Take away this, and it has no sanction at all. But the Church rejecting, always pretends to have acted justly in so doing, and, if so, whereabouts does it confessedly leave the person rejected, if not in a state of damnation? that is to say, if it acknowledge itself to be a Church of Christ, and to have acted justly. If, after all, any particular Church acting thus should refuse the foregoing conclusion, by saying: We meant no such thing concerning the person rejected; we only judged him unworthy of a place among *us,* and therefore put him away, but there are other Churches that may receive him; we would be almost tempted to ask such a Church, if those other Churches be Churches of Christ, and if so, pray what does it account itself? Is it anything more or better than a Church of Christ? And whether, if those other Churches do their duty as faithful Churches, any of them would receive the person it had rejected? If it be answered that, in acting faithfully, none of those other Churches either could or would receive him, then, confessedly, in the judgment of this particular Church, the person ought to be universally rejected; but if otherwise, it condemns itself of having acted unfaithfully, **nay** cruelly, toward a Christian brother, a child of God, in thus rejecting him from the heritage of the Lord, in thus cutting him off from his Father's house, as the unnatural brethren did the beloved Joseph. But even suppose some one or other of those unfaithful Churches should receive the outcast, would their unfaithfulness in so doing nullify, in the judgment of this more faithful Church, its just and faithful. decision in rejecting him? If not, then, confessedly, in its judgment, the person still remains under the influence of its righteous sentence, debarred from the kingdom of heaven; that is to say, if it believe the Scriptures, that what it has righteously done upon earth is ratified in heaven. We see no way that a Church acting *thus* can possibly get rid of this *awful conclusion,* except it acknowledges that the person it has rejected from its communion still has a right to the communion of the Church; but if it acknowledge *this,* whereabout does it leave itself, in thus shutting out a fellow-Christian, an acknowledged brother, a child of God? Do we find any parallel for such conduct in the inspired records, except in the case of Diotrephes, of whom the apostle says, " Who loveth to have the pre-eminence among them, receiveth us not, prating against us with malicious words: and not content therewith, neither doth he himself receive the brethren, and forbiddeth them that would, and casteth them out of the Church."

But further, suppose another Church should receive this castaway, this person which this faithful Church supposed itself to have righteously rejected, would not the Church so doing incur the displeasure, nay even the *censure* of the Church that had rejected him? and, we should think, justly too if he deserved to be rejected. And would not this naturally produce a schism between the Churches? Or, if it be supposed that a schism did already exist, would not this manifestly tend to perpetuate and increase it? If one Church, receiving those whom another puts away, will not be productive of schism, we must confess we cannot tell what would. That Church, therefore, must surely act very schismatically, very unlike a Church of Christ, which necessarily presupposes or produces schism in order to shield an oppressed fellow-Christian from the dreadful consequences of its unrighteous proceedings. And is not this confessedly the case with every Church which rejects a person from its communion while it acknowledges him to be a fellow-Christian; and, in order to excuse this piece of cruelty, says he may find refuge some place else, some other Church may receive him? For, as we have already observed, if no schism did already exist, one Church receiving those whom another has rejected must certainly make one. The same evils also will as justly attach to the conduct of an individual who refuses or breaks communion with a Church because it will not receive or make room for his private opinions or self-devised practices in its public profession and managements; for does he not, in this case, actually take upon him to judge the Church which he thus rejects as unworthy of the communion of Christians? And is not this, to all intents and purposes, declaring it, in his judgment, excommunicate, or at least worthy of excommunication?

Thus have we briefly endeavored to show our brethren what evidently appears to us to be the heinous nature and dreadful consequences of that truly latitudinarian principle and practice which is the bitter root of almost all our divisions, namely, the imposing of our private opinions upon each other as articles of faith or duty, introducing them into the public profession and practice of the Church, and acting upon them as if they were the express law of Christ, by judging and rejecting our brethren that differ from us in those things, or at least by *so* retaining them in our public profession and practice that our brethren cannot join with us, or we with them, without becoming actually partakers in those things which they or we cannot in conscience approve, and which the word of God nowhere expressly enjoins upon us. To cease from all such things, by simply returning to the original standard of Christianity, the profession and practice of the primitive Church, as expressly exhibited upon the sacred page of New Testament scripture, is the only possible way that we can perceive to get rid of those evils. And we humbly think that a uniform agreement in *that* for the preservation of charity would be infinitely preferable to our contentions and divisions; nay, that such a uniformity is the very thing that the Lord requires if the New Testament be a perfect model, a sufficient formula for the worship, discipline, and government of the Christian Church. Let *us* do as we are there expressly told *they* did, say as *they* said; that is, profess and practice as therein expressly enjoined by precept and precedent, in every possible instance, after *their* approved example; and in so doing we shall realize and exhibit all that unity and uniformity that the primitive Church possessed, or that the law of Christ requires. But if, after all, our brethren can point out a better way to regain and preserve that Christian unity and charity expressly enjoined upon the Church of God, we shall thank them for the discovery, and cheerfully embrace it.

Should it still be urged that this would open a wide door to latitudinarianism, seeing all that profess Christianity profess to receive the holy Scriptures, and yet differ so widely in their religious sentiments, we say, let them profess what they will, their difference in religious profession and practice originates in their departure from what is expressly revealed and enjoined, and not in their strict and faithful conformity to it, which is the thing we humbly advise for putting an end to those differences. But you may say, Do they not already all agree in the letter, though differing so far in sentiment? However this may be, have they all agreed to make the letter their rule, or, rather, to make it the subject-matter of their profession and practice? Surely not, or else they would all profess and practice the same thing. Is it not as evident as the shining light that the Scriptures exhibit but one and the self-same subject-matter of profession and practice, at all times and in all places, and that, therefore, to say as it declares, and to do as it prescribes in all its holy precepts, its approved and imitable examples, would unite the Christian Church in a holy sameness of profession and practice throughout the whole world? By the Christian Church throughout the world, we mean the aggregate of such professors as we have described in Propositions 1 and 8, pages 48 and 50, even all that mutually acknowledge each other as Christians, upon the manifest evidence of their faith, holiness, and charity. It is such only we intend when we urge the necessity of Christian unity. Had only such been all along recognized as the genuine subjects of our holy religion, there would not, in all probability, have been so much apparent need for human formulas to preserve an external formality of professional unity and soundness in the faith, but artificial and superficial characters need artificial means to train and unite them. A manifest attachment to our Lord Jesus Christ in faith, holiness, and charity, was the original criterion of Christian character, the distinguishing badge of our holy profession, the foundation and cement of Christian unity. But now, alas! and long since, an external name, a mere educational formality of sameness in the profession of a certain standard or formula of human fabric, with a very moderate degree of what is called morality, forms the bond and foundation, the root and reason of ecclesiastical unity. Take away from such the technicalness of their profession, the shibboleth of party, and what have they more? What have they left to distinguish and hold them together? As for the Bible, they are but little beholden to it, they have learned little from it, they know little about it, and therefore depend as little upon it. Nay, they will even tell you it would be of no use to them without their formula; they could not know a Papist from a Protestant by *it;* that merely by *it* they could neither keep themselves nor the Church right for a single week. You might preach to them what you please, they could not distinguish truth from error. Poor people, it is no wonder they are so fond of their formula! Therefore they that exercise authority upon them and tell them what they are to believe and what they are to do, are called benefactors. These are the reverend and right reverend authors, upon whom they *can* and *do* place a more entire and implicit confidence than upon the holy apostles and prophets; those plain, honest, unassuming men, who would never venture to say or do anything in the name of the Lord without an express revelation from Heaven, and therefore were never distinguished by the venerable titles of Rabbi or Reverend, but just simple Paul, John, Thomas, etc. *These* were but servants. They did not assume to legislate, and, therefore, neither assumed nor received any honorary titles among men, but merely such as were descriptive of their office. And how, we beseech you, shall this gross and prevalent corruption be purged out of the visible professing Church but by a radical reform, but by returning to the original simplicity, the primitive purity of the Christian institution, and, of course, taking up things just as we find them upon the sacred page. And who is there that knows anything of the present state of the Church who does not perceive that it is greatly overrun with the aforesaid evils? Or who that reads his Bible, and receives the impressions it must necessarily produce upon the receptive mind by the statements it exhibits, does not perceive that such a state of things is as distinct from genuine Christianity as oil is from water?

On the other hand, is it not equally as evident that not one of all the erroneous tenets and corrupt practices which have so defamed and corrupted the public profession and practice of Christianity, could ever have appeared in the world had men kept close by the express letter of the Divine law, had they thus held fast that form of sound words contained in the holy Scriptures, and considered it their duty so to do, unless they blame those errors and corruptions upon the very form and expression of the Scriptures, and say that, taken in their letter and connection, they immediately, and at first sight, as it were, exhibit the picture they have drawn. Should any be so bold as to assert this, let them produce their performance, the original is at hand; and let them show us line for line, expression for expression, precept

and precedent for practice, without the torture
of criticism, inference, or conjecture, and then
we shall honestly blame the whole upon the
Bible, and thank those that will give us an
expurged edition of it, call it constitution, or
formula, or what you please, that will not be
liable to lead the simple, unlettered world into
those gross mistakes, those contentions,
schisms, excommunications, and persecutions
which have proved so detrimental and scandalous to our holy religion.

Should it be further objected, that even this
strict literal uniformity would neither infer nor
secure unity of sentiment; it is granted that,
in a certain degree, it would not; nor, indeed,
is there anything either in Scripture or the
nature of things that should induce us to
expect an entire unity of sentiment in the
present imperfect state. The Church may, and
we believe will, come to such a Scriptural unity
of faith and practice, that there will be no
schism in the body, no self-preferring sect of
professed and acknowledged Christians rejecting and excluding their brethren. *This* cannot be, however, till the offensive and excluding causes be removed; and every one knows
what *these* are. But that all the members

should have the same identical views of all Divinely revealed truths, or that there should be no difference of opinion among them, appears to us morally impossible, all things considered. Nor can we conceive what desirable purpose such a unity of sentiment would serve, except to render useless some of those gracious, self-denying, and compassionate precepts of mutual sympathy and forbearance which the word of God enjoins upon his people. Such, then, is the imperfection of our present state. Would to God it might prove, as it ought, a just and humbling counterbalance to our pride! Then, indeed, we would judge one another no more about such matters. We would rather be conscientiously cautious to give no offense; to put no stumbling-block or occasion to fall in our brother's way. We would then no longer exalt our own opinions and inferences to an equality with express revelation, by condemning and rejecting our brother for differing with us in those things.

But although it be granted that the uniformity we plead for would not secure unity of sentiment, yet we should suppose that it would be as efficacious for that purpose as any human expedient or substitute whatsoever.

And here we would ask: Have all or any of those human compilations been able to prevent divisions, to heal breaches, or to produce and maintain unity of sentiment even among those who have most firmly and solemnly embraced them? We appeal for this to the history of all the Churches, and to the present divided state of the Church at large. What good, then, have those devisive expedients accomplished, either to the parties that have adopted them, or to the Church universal, which might not have been as well secured by holding fast in profession and practice that form of sound words contained in the Divine standard, without, at the same time, being liable to any of those dangerous and destructive consequences which have necessarily ensued upon the present mode? Or, will any venture to say that the Scriptures, thus kept in their proper place, would not have been amply sufficient, under the promised influence of the Divine Spirit, to have produced all that unity of sentiment which is necessary to a life of faith and holiness; and also to have preserved the faith and worship of the Church as pure from mixture and error as the Lord intended, or as the present imperfect state of his people can possibly admit? We should tremble to think that any Christian should say that they would not. And if to use them thus would be sufficient for those purposes, why resort to other expedients; to expedients which, from the beginning to this day, have proved utterly insufficient; nay, to expedients which have always produced the very contrary effects, as experience testifies. Let none here imagine that we set any certain limits to the Divine intention, or to the greatness of his power when we thus speak, as if a certain degree of purity from mixture and error were not designed for the Church in this world, or attainable by his people upon earth except in so far as respects the attainment of an angelic or unerring perfection, much less that we mean to suggest that a very moderate degree of unity and purity should content us. We only take it for granted that such a state of perfection is neither intended nor attainable in this world, as will free the Church from all those weaknesses, mistakes, and mismanagements from which she will be completely exempted in heaven, however sound and upright she may now be in her profession, intention, and practice. Neither let any imagine that we here or elsewhere suppose or

intend to assert that human standards are
intentionally set up in competition with the
Bible, much less in opposition to it. We fairly
understand and consider them as human expedients, or as certain doctrinal declarations of
the sense in which the compilers understood
the Scriptures, designed and embraced for the
purpose of promoting and securing that desirable unity and purity which the Bible alone,
without those helps, would be insufficient to
maintain and secure. If this be not the sense
of those that receive and hold them, for the
aforesaid purpose, we should be glad to know
what it is. It is, however, in this very sense
that we take them up when we complain of
them, as not only unsuccessful, but also as
unhappy expedients, producing the very contrary effects. And even suppose it were doubtful whether or not those helps have produced
divisions, one thing, at least, is certain, they
have not been able to prevent them; and now,
that divisions do exist, it is as certain that they
have no fitness nor tendency to heal them, but
the very contrary, as fact and experience
clearly demonstrate. What shall we do, then,
to heal our divisions? We must certainly
take some other way than the present practice,

if they ever be healed; for it expressly says, they must and shall be perpetuated forever. Let all the enemies of Christianity say Amen; but let all Christians continually say: Forbid it, O Lord. May the good Lord subdue the corruptions and heal the divisions of his people. Amen, and amen.

After all that has been said, some of our timid brethren may, possibly, still object, and say: we fear that without the intervention of some definite creed or formula, you will justly incur the censure of latitudinarianism; for how otherwise detect and exclude Arians, Socinians, etc? To such we would reply, that if to profess, inculcate, and practice neither more nor less, neither anything else nor otherwise than the Divine word expressly declares respecting the entire subject of faith and duty, and simply to rest in *that*, as the expression of our faith and rule of our practice, will not amount to the profession and practical exhibition of Arianism, Socinianism, etc., but merely to one and the self-same thing, whatever it may be called, then is the *ground* that we have taken, the *principle* that we advocate, in nowise chargeable with latitudinarianism. Should it be still further objected that all these sects, and many more, profess to receive the Bible, to believe it to be the word of God, and, therefore, will readily profess to believe and practice whatever is revealed and enjoined therein, and yet each will understand it his own way, and of course practice accordingly; nevertheless, according to the plan proposed, you receive them all. We would ask, then, do all these profess and practice neither more nor less than what we read in the Bible — than what is expressly revealed and enjoined therein? If so, they all profess and practice the same thing, for the Bible exhibits but one and the self-same thing to all. Or, is it their own inferences and opinions that they, in reality, profess and practice? If so, then upon the ground that we have taken they stand rejected, as condemned of themselves, for thus professing one thing when in fact and reality they manifestly practice another. But perhaps you will say, that although a uniformity in profession, and it may be in practice too, might thus be produced, yet still it would amount to no more than a mere uniformity in words, and in the external formalities of practice, while the persons thus professing and practicing might each entertain his own sentiments, how different soever these might be. Our reply is, if so, they could hurt nobody but themselves. Besides, if persons thus united professed and practiced all the same things, pray who could tell that they entertained different sentiments, or even in justice suppose it, unless they gave some evident intimation of it? which, if they did, would justly expose them to censure or to rejection, if they repented not; seeing the offense, in this case, must amount to nothing less than an express violation of the expressly revealed will of God — to a manifest transgression of the express letter of the law; for we have declared, that except in such a case, no man, in our judgment, has a right to judge, that is, to condemn or reject his professing brother. Here, we presume, there is no greater latitude assumed or allowed on either side than the law expressly determines. But we would humbly ask, if a professed agreement in the terms of any standard be not liable to the very same objection? If, for instance, Arians, Socinians, Arminians, Calvinists, Antinomians, etc., might not all subscribe the Westminster Confession, the Athanasian Creed, or the doctrinal articles of the Church of England.

If this be denied, we appeal to historical facts; and, in the mean time, venture to assert, that such things are and have been done. Or, will any say, that a person might not with equal ease, honesty, and consistency, be an Arian or a Socinian in his heart while subscribing the Westminister Confession or the Athanasian Creed, as while making his unqualified profession to believe everything that the Scriptures declare concerning Christ? to put all that confidence in him, and to ascribe all that glory, honor, thanksgiving, and praise to him, professed and ascribed to him in the Divine word? If you say not, it follows, of undeniable consequence, that the wisdom of men, in those compilations, has effected what the Divine Wisdom either could not, would not, or did not do, in that all-perfect and glorious revelation of his will, contained in the Holy Scriptures. Happy emendation! Blessed expedient! Happy, indeed, for the Church that Athanasius arose in the fourth century to perfect what the holy apostles and prophets had left in such a rude and unfinished state. But if, after all, the Divine Wisdom did not think proper to do anything more, or anything else than is already done in the sacred oracles, to settle and determine those important points, who can say that he determined such a thing should be done afterward? Or has he anywhere given us any intimation of such an intention?

Let it here be carefully observed that the question before us is about human standards designed to be subscribed, or otherwise solemnly acknowledged, for the preservation of ecclesiastical unity and purity, and therefore, of course, by no means applies to the many excellent performances, for the Scriptural elucidation and defense of Divinely revealed truths and other instructive purposes. These, we hope, according to their respective merit, we as highly esteem, and as thankfully receive, as our brethren. But further, with respect to unity of sentiment, even suppose it ever so desirable, it appears highly questionable whether such a thing can at all be secured, by any expedient whatsoever, especially if we consider that it necessarily presupposes in so far a unity or sameness of understanding. Or, will any say, that from the youth of seventeen to the man of fourscore — from the illiterate peasant, up to the learned prelate — all the legitimate members of the Church entertain the same sentiments under their respective formulas? If not, it is still but a mere verbal agreement, a mere show of unity. They say an amen to the same forms of speech, or of sound words, as they are called, without having, at the same time, the same views of the subject; or, it may be, without any determinate views of it at all. And, what is still worse, this profession is palmed upon the world, as well as upon the too credulous professors themselves, for unity of sentiment, for soundness in the faith; when in a thousand instances, they have, properly speaking, no faith at all; that is to say, if faith necessarily presupposes a true and satisfactory conviction of the Scriptural evidence and certainty of the truth of the propositions we profess to believe. A cheap and easy orthodoxy this, to which we may attain by committing to memory a catechism, or professing our approbation of a formula, made ready to our hand, which we may or may not have once read over; or even if we have, yet may not have been able to read it so correctly and intelligently as to clearly understand one single paragraph from beginning to end, much less to compare it with, to search and try it by the holy Scriptures, to see

if these things be so. A cheap and easy orthodoxy this, indeed, to which a person may thus
attain, without so much as turning over a
single leaf of his Bible, whereas Christ knew
no other way of leading us to the knowledge
of himself, at least has prescribed no other,
but by searching the Scriptures, with reliance
upon his Holy Spirit. A person may, however, by this short and easy method, become
as orthodox as the apostle Paul (if such superficial professions, such mere hearsay verbal
repetitions can be called orthodoxy) without
ever once consulting the Bible, or so much as
putting up a single petition for the Holy Spirit
to guide him into all truth, to open his understanding to know the Scriptures; for, his form
of sound words truly believed, if it happen to
be right, must, without more ado, infallibly
secure his orthodoxy. Thrice happy expedient! But is there no latitudinarianism in all
this? Is not this taking a latitude, in devising
ways and means for accomplishing Divine and
saving purposes, which the Divine law has
nowhere prescribed, for which the Scriptures
nowhere afford us either precept or precedent?
Unless it can be shown that making human
standards to determine the doctrine, worship,

discipline, and government of the Church for the purpose of preserving her unity and purity, and requiring an approbation of them as a term of communion is a Scripture institution. Far be it from us, in the mean time, to allege that the Church should not make every Scriptural exertion in her power to preserve her unity and purity; to teach and train up her members in the knowledge of all divinely revealed truth; or to say that the evils above complained of attach to all that are in the habit of using the aforesaid helps; or that this wretched state of things, however general, necessarily proceeds from the legitimate use of such; but rather and entirely from the abuse of them, which is the very and only thing that we are all along opposing when we allude to those subordinate standards. (An appellation this, by the by, which appears to us highly paradoxical, if not utterly inconsistent, and full of confusion.)

But, however this may be, we are by no means to be understood as at all wishing to deprive our fellow-Christians of any necessary and possible assistance to understand the Scriptures, or to come to a distinct and particular knowledge of every truth they contain, for

which purpose the Westminster Confession
and Catechisms may, with many other excellent performances, prove eminently useful.
But, having served ourselves of these, let our
profiting appear to all, by our manifest
acquaintance with the Bible; by making our
profession of faith and obedience; by declaring its Divine dictates, in which we acquiesce,
as the subject-matter and rule of both; in our
ability to take the Scripture in its connection
upon these subjects, so as to understand one
part of it by the assistance of another; and in
manifesting our self-knowledge, our knowledge of the way of salvation and of the mystery of the Christian life, in the express light
of Divine revelation, by a direct and immediate reference to, and correct repetition of
what it declares upon those subjects. We take
it for granted that no man either knows God,
or himself, or the way of salvation, but in so
far as he has heard and understood his voice
upon those subjects, as addressed to him in
the Scriptures, and that, therefore, whatever
he has heard and learned of a saving nature,
is contained in the express terms of the Bible.
If so, in the express terms, in and by which
" he hath heard and learned of the Father,"

let him declare it. This by no means forbids
him to use helps, but, we humbly presume, will
effectually prevent him from resting either in
them or upon them, which is the evil so justly
complained of; from taking up with the directory instead of the object to which it directs.
Thus will the whole subject of his faith and
duty, in so far as he has attained, be expressly
declared in a " Thus saith the Lord."   And is
it not worthy of remark, that of whatever use
other books may be, to direct and lead us to
the Bible, or to prepare and assist us to understand it, yet the Bible never directs us to any
book but itself.   When we come forward, then,
as Christians, to be received by the Church,
which, properly speaking, has but one book,
" For to it were committed the oracles of
God," let us hear of none else.   Is it not upon
the credible profession of our faith in, and
obedience to its Divine contents, that the
Church is bound to receive applicants for
admission?   And does not a profession of our
faith and obedience necessarily presuppose a
knowledge of the dictates we profess to believe
and obey?   Surely, then, we can declare them,
and as surely, if our faith and obedience be
Divine, as to the subject-matter, rule, and rea-

son of them, it must be a "Thus saith the
Lord"; if otherwise, they are merely human,
being taught by the precepts of men. In the
case then before us, that is, examination for
Church-membership, let the question no longer
be, What does any human system say of the
primitive or present state of man? of the person, offices, and relations of Christ, etc., etc.?
or of this, that, or the other duty? but, What
says the Bible? Were this mode of procedure
adopted, how much better acquainted with
their Bibles would Christians be? What an
important alteration would it also make in the
education of youth? Would it not lay all
candidates for admission into the Church
under the happy necessity of becoming particularly acquainted with the holy Scriptures?
whereas, according to the present practice,
thousands know little about them.

One thing still remains that may appear
matter of difficulty or objection to some,
namely, that such a close adherence to the
express letter of the Divine word, as we seem
to propose, for the restoration and mainte-
nance of Christian unity, would not only interfere with the free communication of our
sentiments one to another upon religious sub-

jects, but must, of course, also necessarily interfere with the public preaching and expounding of the Scriptures for the edification of the Church. Such as feel disposed to make this objection, should justly consider that one of a similar nature, and quite as plausible, might be made to the adoption of human standards, especially when made as some of them confessedly are, " the standard for all matters of doctrine, worship, discipline, and government." In such a case it might, with as much justice, at least, be objected to the adopters: You have now no more use for the Bible; you have got another book, which you have adopted as a standard for all religious purposes; you have no further use for explaining the Scriptures, either as to matter of faith or duty, for this you have confessedly done already in your standard, wherein you have determined all matters of this nature. You also profess to hold fast the form of sound words, which you have thus adopted, and therefore you must never open your mouth upon any subject in any other terms than those of your standard. In the mean time, would any of the parties which has thus adopted its respective standard, consider any of these charges just? If not, let them do as they would be done by. We must confess, however, that for our part, we cannot see how, with any shadow of consistency, some of them could clear themselves, especially of the first; that is to say, if words have any determinate meaning; for certainly it would appear almost, if not altogether incontrovertible, that a book adopted by any party as its standard for all matters of doctrine, worship, discipline, and government, must be considered as the Bible of that party. And after all that can be said in favor of such a performance, be it called Bible, standard, or what it may, it is neither anything more nor better than the judgment or opinion of the party composing or adopting it, and, therefore, wants the sanction of a Divine authority, except in the opinion of the party which has thus adopted it. But can the opinion of any party, be it ever so respectable, give the stamp of a Divine authority to its judgments? If not, then every human standard is deficient in this leading, all-important, and indispensable property of a rule or standard for the doctrine, worship, discipline, and government of the Church of God. But, without insisting further upon the intrinsic and irremediable deficiency of human standards for the above purpose (which is undeniably evident if it be granted that a Divine authority is indispensably necessary to constitute a standard or rule for Divine things, such as is the constitution and managements, the faith, and worship of the Christian Church), we would humbly ask, Would any of the parties consider as just the foregoing objections, however conclusive and well founded all or any of them may appear? We believe they would not. And may we not with equal consistency hold fast the expressly revealed will of God, in the very terms in which it is expressed in his holy word, as the very expression of our faith and express rule of our duty, and yet take the same liberty that they do, notwithstanding their professed and steadfast adherence to their respective standards? We find they do not cease to expound, because they have already expounded, as before alleged, nor yet do they always confine themselves to the express terms of their respective standards, yet they acknowledge them to be their standards and profess to hold them fast. Yea, moreover, some of them profess, and, if we may conclude from facts, we believe each of them is disposed to defend by occasional vindications (or testimonies, as some call them) the sentiments they have adopted and engrossed in their standards, without at the same time requiring an approbation of those occasional performances as a term of communion. And what should hinder us, or any, adopting the Divine standard, as aforesaid, with equal consistency to do the same for the vindication of the Divine truths expressly revealed and enjoined therein? To say that we can not believe and profess the truth, understand one another, inculcate and vindicate the faith and law of Christ, or do the duties incumbent upon Christians or a Christian Church without a human standard, is not only saying that such a standard is quite essential to the very being of Christianity, and, of course, must have existed before a Church was or could be formed, but it is also saying, that without such a standard, the Bible would be quite inadequate as a rule of faith and duty, or, rather, of no use at all, except to furnish materials for such a work; whereas the Church of Ephesus, long before we have any account of the existence of such a standard, is not only mentioned, with many others, as in a state of existence, and of high attainments too, but is also commended for her vigilance and fidelity in detecting and rejecting false apostles. " Thou hast tried them which say they are apostles, and are not, and hast found them liars." But should any pretend to say that although such performances be not essential to the very being of the Church, yet are they highly conducive to its wellbeing and perfection. For the confutation of such an assertion, we would again appeal to Church history and existing facts and leave the judicious and intelligent Christian to determine.

If after all that has been said, any should still pretend to affirm that the plan we profess to adopt and recommend is truly latitudinarian, in the worst and fullest sense of the term, inasmuch as it goes to make void all human efforts to maintain the unity and purity of the Church, by substituting a vague and indefinite approbation of the Scriptures as an alternative for creeds, confessions, and testimonies, and thereby opens a wide door for the reception of all sorts of characters and opinions into the Church. Were we not convinced by experience, that notwithstanding all that has been said, such objections would likely be made, or

that some weak persons might possibly consider them as good as demonstration, especially
when proceeding from highly influential characters (and there have not been wanting such
in all ages to oppose, under various plausible
pretenses, the unity and peace of the Church),
were it not for these considerations, we should
content ourselves with what we have already
advanced upon the whole of the subject, as
being well assured *that* duly attended to, there
would not be the least room for such an objection; but to prevent if possible such unfounded
conclusions, or if this cannot be done, to
caution and assist the too credulous and
unwary professor, that he may not be carried
away all at once with the high-toned confidence of bold assertion, we would refer him
to the overture for union in truth contained
in the foregoing address. Union in truth,
among all the manifest subjects of grace and
truth, is what we advocate. We carry our
views of union no further than *this,* nor do we
presume to recommend it upon any other
principle than truth alone. Now, surely, truth
is something certain and definite; if not, who
will take upon him to define and determine it?
This we suppose God has sufficiently done

already in his holy word. That men therefore truly receive and make the proper use of the Divine word for walking together in truth and peace, in holiness and charity, is, no doubt, the ardent desire of all the genuine subjects of our holy religion. This, we see, however, they have not done, to the awful detriment and manifest subversion of what we might almost call the primary intention of Christianity. We dare not, therefore, follow their example, nor adopt their ruinous expedients. But does it therefore follow that Christians may not, or can not take proper steps to ascertain that desirable and preceptive unity which the Divine word requires and enjoins? Surely no; at least we have supposed no such thing; but, on the contrary, have overtured to our brethren what appears to us undeniably just and Scripturally evident, and which, we humbly think, if adopted and acted upon, would have the desired effect; adopted and acted upon, not indeed as a standard for the doctrine, worship, discipline, and government of the Church, for it pretends not to determine these matters, but rather supposes the existence of a fixed and certain standard of Divine original, in which everything that the wisdom of God saw meet to reveal and determine, for *these* and all other purposes, is expressly defined and determined; between the Christian and which, no medium of human determination ought to be interposed. In all this there is surely nothing like the denial of any lawful effort to promote and maintain the Church's unity, though there be a refusal of the unwarrantable interposition of an unauthorized and assuming power.

Let none imagine that we are here determining upon the merits of the overture to which, in the case before us, we find it necessary to appeal in our own defense against the injustice of the supposed charge above specified. To the judgment of our brethren have we referred that matter, and with them we leave it. All we intend, therefore, is to avail ourselves so far of what we have done, as to show that we have no intention whatsoever of substituting a vague indefinite approbation of the Scriptures as an alternative for creeds, confessions, and testimonies, for the purpose of restoring the Church to her original constitutional unity and purity. In avoiding Scylla we would cautiously guard against being wrecked upon Charybdis. Extremes, we are told, are dangerous. We therefore suppose a middle way, a safe way, so plainly marked out by unerring wisdom, that if duly attended to under the Divine direction, the wayfaring men, though fools, need not err therein, and of such is the kingdom of God: "For he hath chosen the foolish things of the world to confound the things that are wise." We therefore conclude it must be a plain way, a way most graciously and most judiciously adapted to the capacity of the subjects, and consequently not the way of subscribing or otherwise approving human standards as a term of admission into his Church, as a test and defense of orthodoxy, which even the compilers themselves are not always agreed about, and which nineteen out of twenty of the Lord's people cannot thoroughly understand. It must be a way very far remote from logical subtilties and metaphysical speculations, and as such we have taken it up, upon the plainest and most obvious principles of Divine revelation and common sense — the common sense, we mean, of Christians, exercised upon the plainest and most obvious truths and facts divinely recorded for their instruction. Hence we have supposed, in the first place, the true discrimination of Christian character to consist in an intelligent profession of our faith in Christ and obedience to him in all things according to the Scriptures, the reality of which profession is manifested by the holy consistency of the tempers and conduct of the professors with the express dictates and approved examples of the Divine word. Hence we have humility, faith, piety, temperance, justice, charity, etc., professed and manifested, in the first instance, by the persons professing with self-application the convincing, humbling, encouraging, pious, temperate, just and charitable doctrines and precepts of the inspired volume, as exhibited and enforced in its holy and approved examples, and the sincerity of this profession evidently manifested by the consistency of the professor's temper and conduct with the entire subject of his profession, either by an irreprovable conformity, like good Zachariah and Elisabeth, which is of all things most desirable, or otherwise, in case of any visible failure, by an apparently sincere repentance and evident reformation. Such professors, and such only, have we supposed to be, by common consent, truly worthy the Christian name. Ask from the one end of heaven to the other, the whole number of such intelligent and consistent professors as we intend and have described, and, we humbly presume, there will not be found one dissenting voice. They will all acknowledge, with one consent, that the true discrimination of Christian character consists in these things, and that the radical or manifest want of any of the aforesaid properties completely destroys the character.

We have here only taken for granted what we suppose no rational professor will venture to deny; namely: that the Divine word contains an ample sufficiency upon every one of the foregoing topics to stamp the above character, if so be that the impressions which its express declarations are obviously calculated to produce be truly received; for instance, suppose a person profess to believe, with application to himself, that whole description of human depravity and wretchedness which the Scriptures exhibit of fallen man, in the express declarations and dismal examples of human wickedness therein recorded, contrasted with the holy nature, the righteous requirements, and inflexible justice of an infinitely holy, just, and jealous God, would not the subject-matter of such a profession be amply sufficient to impress the believing mind with the most profound humility, self-abhorrence, and dreadful apprehension of the tremendous effects of sin? Again, should the person profess to believe, in connection with this, all that the Scriptures declare of the sovereign love, mercy, and condescension of God toward guilty, depraved, rebellious man, as the same is manifested in Christ, and in all the gracious declarations, invitations, and promises that are made in and through him for the relief and encouragement of the guilty, etc., would not all this, taken together, be sufficient to impress the believing mind with the most lively confidence, gratitude, and love? Should this person, moreover, profess that delight and confidence in the Divine Redeemer — that voluntary submission to him — that worship and adoration of him which the Scriptures expressly declare to have been the habits and practice of his people, would not the subject-matter of this profession be amply sufficient to impress the believing mind with that dutiful disposition, with that gracious veneration and supreme reverence which the word of God requires? And should not all this taken together satisfy the Church, in so far, in point of profession? If not, there is no alternative but a new revelation; seeing that to deny this, is to assert that a distinct perception and sincere profession of whatever the word declares upon every point of faith and duty, is not only insufficient, as a doctrinal means, to produce a just and suitable impression in the mind of the believing subject, but is also insufficient to satisfy the Church as to a just and adequate profession; if otherwise, then it will necessarily follow, that not every sort of character, but that one sort only, is admissible upon the principle we have adopted; and that by the universal consent of all that we, at least, dare venture to call Christians, *this* is acknowledged to be, exclusively, the true Christian character. Here, then, we have a fixed point, a certain description of character, which combines in every professing subject the Scriptural profession, the evident manifestation of humility, faith, piety, temperance, justice, and charity, instructed by, and evidently answering to the entire declaration of the word upon each of those topics, which, as so many properties, serve to constitute the character. Here, we say, we have a fixed, and at the same time sweeping distinction, which, as of old, mani-

festly divides the whole world, however otherwise distinguished, into but two classes only.
" We know," said the apostle, evidently speaking of such, " that we are of God, and the
whole world lieth in wickedness."

Should it be inquired concerning the persons
included in this description of character,
whether they be Arminians or Calvinists, or
both promiscuously huddled together? It may
be justly replied, that according to what we
have proposed, they can be nominally neither,
and of course not both, for we call no man
master on earth, for one is our Master, even
Christ, and all we are brethren, are Christians
by profession; and as such abstract specula-
tion and argumentative theory make no part
either of our profession or practice. Such
professors, then, as we intend and have described, are just what their profession and
practice make them to be; and this we hope
has been Scripturally, and we might add, satisfactorily defined, in so far, at least, as the
limits of so brief a performance would admit.
We also entertain the pleasing confidence that
the plan of procedure which we have ventured
to suggest, if duly attended to, if fully reduced
to practice, would necessarily secure to the

professing subject all the advantages of
divinely revealed truth, without any liability
to conceal, to diminish, or to misrepresent it,
as it goes immediately to ascribe everything
to God respecting his sovereignty, independence, power, wisdom, goodness, justice, truth,
holiness, mercy, condescension, love, and
grace, etc., which is ascribed to him in his
word, as also to receive whatever it declares
concerning the absolute dependence of the
poor, guilty, depraved, polluted creature, upon
the Divine will, power, and grace for every
saving purpose; a just perception and cor-
respondent profession of which, according to
the Scriptures, is supposed to constitute that
fundamental ingredient in Christian character:
true evangelical humility. And so of the rest.
Having thus, we hope, Scripturally and evidently determined the character, with the proper mode of ascertaining it, to the satisfaction
of all concerned, we next proceed to affirm,
with the same Scriptural evidence, that among
such, however situated, whether in the same
or similar associations, there ought to be no
schisms, no uncharitable divisions, but that
they ought all mutually to receive and acknowledge each other as brethren. As to the

truth of this assertion, they are all likewise
agreed, without one dissenting voice. We
next suggest that for this purpose they ought
all to walk by the same rule, to mind and
speak the same thing, etc., and that this rule is,
and ought to be, the Divine standard. Here
again we presume there can be no objection;
no, not a single dissenting voice. As to the
rule itself, we have ventured to allege that the
New Testament is the proper and immediate
rule, directory, and formula for the New Testament Church, and for the particular duties of
Christians, as the Old Testament was for the
Old Testament Church, and for the particular
duties of the subject under that dispensation;
at the same time by no means excluding the
Old as fundamental to, illustrative of, and
inseparably connected with the New, and as
being every way of equal authority, as well as
of an entire sameness with it in every point of
moral natural duty, though not immediately our
rule, without the intervention and coincidence
of the New, in which our Lord has taught
his people, by the ministry of his holy apostles,
all things whatsoever they should observe and
do, till the end of the world. Thus we come
to the one rule, taking the Old Testament as

explained and perfected by the New, and the New as illustrated and enforced by the Old; assuming the latter as the proper and immediate directory for the Christian Church, as also for the positive and particular duties of Christians as to all things whatsoever they should observe and do. Further, that in the observance of this Divine rule, this authentic and infallible directory, all such may come to the desirable coincidence of holy unity and uniformity of profession and practice, we have overtured that they all speak, profess, and practice the very same things that are exhibited upon the sacred page of New Testament Scripture, as spoken and done by the Divine appointment and approbation; and that this be extended to every possible instance of uniformity, without addition or diminution, without introducing anything of private opinion or doubtful disputation into the public profession or practice of the Church. Thus and thus have we overtured to all intents and purposes, as may be clearly seen by consulting the overture itself; in which, however, should anything appear not sufficiently explicit, we flatter ourselves it may be fully understood by taking into consideration what has been variously suggested upon this important subject throughout the whole of these premises; so that if any due degree of attention be paid, we should think it next to impossible that we could be so far misunderstood as to be charged with latitudinarianism in any usual sense of the word. Here we have proposed but one description of character as eligible, or, indeed, as at all admissible to the rights and privileges of Christianity. This description of character we have defined by certain and distinguishing properties, which not only serve to distinguish it from every other, but in which all the real subjects themselves are agreed, without one exception, all such being mutually and reciprocally acknowledged by each other as legitimate members of the Church of God. All these, moreover, agreeing in the indispensable obligation of their unity, and in the one rule by which it is instructed, and also in the preceptive necessity of an entire uniformity in their public profession and managements for promoting and preserving this unity, that there should be no schism in the body, but that all the members should have the same care one for another; yet in many instances, unhappily, and, we may truly say, involuntarily differing through mistake and mismanagement, which it is our humble desire and endeavor to detect and remove, by obviating everything that causeth difference, being persuaded that as truth is one and indivisible wherever it exists, so all the genuine subjects of it, if disentangled from artificial impediments, must and will necessarily fall in together, be all on one side, united in one profession, acknowledge each other as brethren, and love as children of the same family. For this purpose we have overtured a certain and determinate application of the rule, to which we presume there can be no reasonable objection, and which, if adopted and acted upon, must, we think, infallibly produce the desired effect; unless we should suppose that to say and do what is expressly said and done before our eyes upon the sacred page, would offend the believer, or that a strict uniformity, an entire Scriptural sameness in profession and practice, would produce divisions and offenses among those who are already united in one spirit, one Lord, one faith, one baptism, one hope of their calling, and in one God and Father of all, who is above all, and through all, and in them all, as is confessedly the case with all of this character throughout all the Churches. To induce to this we have also attempted to call their attention to the heinous nature and awful consequences of schism, and to that evil anti-scriptural principle from which it necessarily proceeds. We have likewise endeavored to show, we humbly think with demonstrable evidence, that there is no alternative but either to adopt that Scriptural uniformity we have recommended, or else continue as we are, bewildered in schisms and overwhelmed with the accursed evils inseparable from such a state. It remains now with our brethren to determine upon the whole of these premises, to adopt or to reject, as they see cause; but, in the mean time, let none impeach us with the latitudinarian expedient of substituting a vague, indefinite approbation of the holy Scriptures as an alternative for the present practice of making the approbation of human standards a term of communion; as it is undeniably evident that nothing can be further from our intention. Were we to judge of what we humbly propose and urge as indispensably necessary for the reformation and unity of the Church, we should rather apprehend that there was reason to fear a charge of a very different nature; namely: that we aimed at too much strictness, both as to the description of character which we say ought only to be admitted, and also as to the use and application of the rule. But should this be the case, we shall cheerfully bear with it, as being fully satisfied that not only the common sentiment of all apparently sincere, intelligent, and practical Christians is on our side, but that also the plainest and most ample testimonies of the inspired volume sufficiently attest the truth and propriety of what we plead for, as essential to the Scriptural unity and purity of the Christian Church, and this, we humbly presume, is what we should incessantly aim at. It would be strange, indeed, if, in contending earnestly for the faith once delivered to the saints, we should overlook those fruits of righteousness, that manifest humility, piety, temperance, justice, and charity, without which faith itself is dead, being alone. We trust we have not so learned Christ; if so be we have been taught by him as the truth is in Jesus, we must have learned a very different lesson indeed. While we would, therefore, insist upon an entire conformity to the Scriptures in profession, that we might all believe and speak the same things, and thus be perfectly joined together in the same mind and in the same judgment, we would, with equal scrupulosity, insist upon and look for an entire conformity to them in practice, in all those whom we acknowledge as our brethren in Christ. " By their fruits ye shall know them." " Not every one that saith unto me, Lord, Lord, shall enter into the kingdom of heaven; but he that doeth the will of my Father which is in heaven. Therefore whosoever heareth those sayings of mine, and doeth them not, shall be likened unto a foolish man which built his house upon the sand. Woe unto you scribes and Pharisees, hypocrites, for ye say and do not." We therefore conclude that to advocate unity alone, however desirable in itself, without at the same time purging the Church of apparently unsanctified characters, even of all that cannot show their faith by their works, would be, at best, but a poor, superficial, skin-deep reformation. It is from such characters, then, as the proposed reformation, if carried into effect, would entirely deprive of a name and a place in the Church, that we have the greatest reason to apprehend a determined and obstinate opposition. And alas! there are very many of this description, and in many places, of considerable influence. But neither should this discourage us, when we consider the expressly revealed will of God upon this point, Ezek. xliv: 6, 9, with Matt. xiii: 15, 17; 1 Cor. v: 6, 13, with many other scriptures. Nor, in the end, will the multitude of unsanctified professors which the proposed reformation would necessarily exclude, have any reason to rejoice in the unfaithfulness of those that either through ignorance, or for filthy lucre sake, indulged them with a name and place in the Church of God. These unfaithful stewards, these now mistaken friends, will one day be considered by such as their most cruel and treacherous enemies. These, then, are our sentiments upon the entire subject of Church-reformation; call it latitudinarianism, or Puritanism. or what you please; and *this* is the reformation for which we plead. Thus, upon the whole, have we briefly attempted to point out those evils, and to prevent those mistakes which we earnestly desire to see obviated for the general peace, welfare, and prosperity of the Church of God. Our dear brethren, giving credit to our sincere and well-meant intention, will charitably excuse the imperfections of our humble performance, and by the assistance of their better judgment correct those mistakes, and supply those deficiencies which in a first attempt of this nature may have escaped our notice. We are sorry, in the mean time, to have felt a necessity of approaching so near the borders of controversy, by briefly attempting to answer objections which we plainly foresaw would, through mistake or prejudice, be made against our proceedings; controversy making no part of our intended plan. But such objections and surmises having already reached our ears from different quarters, we thought it necessary to attend to them, that, by so doing, we might not only prevent mistakes, but also save our friends the trouble of entering into verbal disputes in order to remove them, and thus prevent, as much as possible, that most unhappy of all practices sanctioned by the plausible pretense of zeal for the truth — religious controversy among professors. We would, therefore, humbly advise our friends to concur with us in our professed and sincere intention to avoid this evil practice. Let it suffice to put into the hands of such as desire information what we hereby publish for that purpose. If this, however, should not satisfy, let them give in their objections in writing; we shall thankfully receive, and seriously consider, with all due attention, whatever comes before us in this way; but verbal controversy we absolutely refuse. Let none imagine that by so saying, we mean to dissuade Christians from affording all the assistance they can to each other as humble inquirers after truth. To decline this friendly office would be to refuse the performance of an important duty. But certainly there is a manifest difference between speaking the truth in love for the edification of our brethren, and attacking each other with a spirit of controversial hostility, to confute and prove each other wrong. We believe it is rare to find one instance of this kind of arguing that does not terminate in bitterness. Let us, therefore, cautiously avoid it. Our Lord says, Matt. xvii: 7: "Woe unto the world because of offenses." Scott, in his incomparable work lately published in this country, called his Family Bible, observes in his notes upon this place, "that our Lord here intends all these evils within the Church which prejudice men's minds against his religion, or any doctrines of it. The scandalous lives, horrible oppressions, cruelties, and iniquities of men called Christians; their divisions and bloody contentions; their idolatries and superstitions, are at this day the *great offenses* and *causes of stumbling* to Jews, Mohammedans, and pagans in all the four quarters of the globe, and they furnish infidels of every description with their most dangerous weapons against the truth. The acrimonious controversies agitated among those who agree in the principal doctrines of the Gospel, and their mutual contempt and revilings of each other, together with the extravagant notions and wicked practices found among them, form the grand prejudice in the minds of multitudes against evangelical religion, and harden the hearts of heretics, Pharisees, disguised infidels, and careless sinners against the truths of the Gospel. In these and numberless other ways, it may be said: 'Woe unto the world because of offenses,' for the devil, the sower of these tares, makes use of them in deceiving the nations of the earth and in murdering the souls of men. In the present state of human nature, it must needs be that such offenses should intervene, and God has wise and righteous reasons for permitting them; yet we should consider it as the greatest of evils to be accessory to the destruction of souls; and an awful woe is denounced against every one whose delusions or crimes thus stumble men and set them against the only method of salvation." We conclude with an extract from the Boston Anthology, which, with too many of the same kind that might be adduced, furnish a mournful comment upon the text; we mean, upon the sorrowful subject of our woful divisions and corruptions. The following reply to the Rev. Mr. Cram, missionary from Massachusetts to the Senecas, was made by the principal chiefs and warriors of the six nations in council assembled at Buffalo creek, State of New York, in the presence of the agent of the United States for Indian affairs, in the summer of 1805. "I am come, brethren," said the missionary, "to enlighten your minds and to instruct you how to worship the Great Spirit agreeably to his will, and to preach to you the Gospel of his Son Jesus Christ. There is but one way to serve God, and if you do not embrace the right way, you cannot be happy hereafter." To which they reply: "Brother, we understand that your religion is written in a book. You say that there is but one way to worship and serve the Great Spirit. If there be but one religion, why do you white people differ so much about it? Why not all agree as you can all read the book? Brother, we do not understand these things. We are told your religion was given to your forefathers; we, also, have a religion which was given to our forefathers; it teaches us to be *thankful* for all the favors we receive; to *love* one another, and to be *united*. We never quarrel about religion. We are told you have been preaching to the white people in this place. Those people are our neighbors, we are acquainted with them. We will wait a little to see what effect your preaching has upon *them*. If we find it does them good, makes them *honest,* and *less* disposed to cheat Indians, we will then consider again of what you have said." Thus closed the conference. Alas, poor people! how do our divisions and corruptions stand in your way! What a pity that you find us not upon original ground, such as the apostles left the primitive Churches! Had we but exhibited to you their unity and charity; their humble, honest, and affectionate deportment toward each other and toward all men, you would not have had those evil and shameful things to object to our holy religion, and to prejudice your minds against it. But your conversion, it seems, awaits our reformation; awaits our return to primitive unity and love. To this may the God of mercy speedily restore us, both for your sakes and our own, that *his way* may be known upon earth, and his saving health among all nations. Let the people praise thee, O God; let all the people praise thee. Amen, and amen.

THE END.

Introduction to the Sermon on the Law

ALEXANDER CAMPBELL was born September 12, 1788, in the County of Antrim, Ireland. His father was Thomas Campbell, of Scotch descent, and his mother was Jane Carneigle, of French Huguenot descent. He was brought up in a Seceder Presbyterian minister's home, characterized by a simple yet fervent devotion to all the requirements of religious instruction peculiar to that church. His early education was obtained partly under the instruction of his father and partly under that of his uncles. He was designed for the ministry by his father and was quietly urged in that direction through all his early training. The boy, however, did not show any peculiar leaning toward the ministry or any aptitude for serious study until he was fifteen or sixteen years of age. It was sometime after the father became pastor of the church at Ahorey that the son passed through a religious experience accepted as conversion, and was received as a member of the church. He began to take interest in religious questions and made more rapid progress in his studies. His father made him assistant in the academy at Rich Hill, and so efficient was his service that when he took the journey to America he left the affairs of the academy largely in the son's care.

Very soon after the arrival of the father in America he sent for his family to join him. Preparations were made for emigrating, and the family set sail. The ship was wrecked on an island on the coast of Scotland. This happened in October, 1808. Since it was thought unsafe to attempt the voyage across the Atlantic so late in the year, the family decided to spend the winter in Glasgow, in order that Alexander might have the advantages of the university. The year spent there was notable in the change it wrought in the religious views of the young man. He broke finally with the Seceder Church without knowing that his father had done likewise in America. He supposed the knowledge of the fact would be a source of sorrow to his father, but to his surprise and delight when he arrived in western Pennsylvania with the family in the fall of 1809, he found that his father had taken an even more radical and momentous course than himself. The proof sheets of the "Declaration and Address" were just coming from press when the family joined the father. The son found himself in hearty accord with the ideas and principles of his father. He was then but twenty-one years of age, but had on the occasion of the shipwreck dedicated himself to the work of preaching the Gospel. He began immediately to advocate in private and public the cause of the "Christian Association of Washington." Within a year he was put forward to defend in public discourse the principles of the Association against the attack of its critics. He manifested such power and capacity for leadership in his public discourses that he was at once accepted as the destined leader of the movement. The foundations were laid by the father: the son arrived upon the scene in time to commence work upon the superstructure.

From the beginning the movement was given a Baptistward direction by the application of the principle, "Where the Scriptures speak, we speak; where they are silent, we are silent," to the question of infant baptism. It was not found mentioned or practiced in the apostolic church, hence it must not be named in the new community. Only the baptism of believers would be practiced. The application of the principles to all items of religious faith and practice was forced upon them after they were driven to convert the "Christian Association" into a regularly organized church, in 1810.

An investigation of the New Testament as to the form of baptism convinced Alexander Campbell that he had not been properly baptized. He and his wife applied to a Baptist minister to perform the service. He had settled upon this step before informing his father. When he informed him of his purpose, the father and all the members of his family decided to be immersed at the same time. This brought them into sympathetic relations with the Baptists. After repeated invitations to enter the fellowship of Baptist churches, they finally did so in 1813. From the beginning of this union the Campbells held views upon several subjects opposed to Baptist views. One of these subjects was as to the relative authority of the Old and New Testaments. They held, as is recorded in their writings as early as 1811, that the New Testament alone was of authority for Christian faith and practice. Along with this went an apparent minimizing of the value of the Old Testament, which was new and unwelcome to Baptist ears. There were some Baptists in the Redstone Association of Pennsylvania, to which the Campbells belonged, who opposed the union at first, and never ceased agitation against them. This opposition came to an open demonstration in 1816 at an annual meeting of the Association at Cross Creek, Virginia. Alexander Campbell had become by this time a preacher of unusual power and great popularity with the people. Many were anxious to hear him at the meeting of the Association, though no place had been assigned him on the program, but some were determined that he should not be heard. One of the speakers was taken ill, and Mr. Campbell was called upon to take his place. He preached a sermon from the text, Romans 8:3. It became known as "The Sermon on the Law." Great offense was given the opponents of the Campbells by the sentiments of this sermon. They began a public opposition against them which finally led to their withdrawal from the Redstone Association, and their union with the Mahoning Association of

Ohio. The ideas set forth in the sermon, so offensive to the Baptists of the time, are generally accepted to-day, even by Baptists themselves.

ALEXANDER CAMPBELL.

Sermon on the Law

REQUESTS have occasionally, during several years, been made for the publication, in this work, of a discourse on the Law, pronounced by me at a meeting of the Regular Baptist Association, on Cross Creek, Virginia, 1816. Recently these requests have been renewed with more earnestness; and, although much crowded for room, I have concluded to comply with the wishes of my friends. It was rather a youthful performance, and is in one particular, to my mind, long since exceptionable. Its views of the atonement are rather commercial than evangelical. But this was only casually introduced and does not affect the object of the discourse on the merits of the great question discussed in it. I thought it better to let it go to the public again without the change of a sentiment in it. Although precisely thirty years this month since I delivered it, and some two or three years after my union with the Baptist denomination, the intelligent reader will discover in it the elements of things which have characterized all our writings on the sub-

ject of modern Christianity from that day to
the present.

But as this discourse was, because of its alleged heterodoxy by the Regular Baptist
Association, made the ground of my impeach-
ment and trial for heresy at its next annual
meeting, it is as an item of ecclesiastic history interesting. It was by a great effort on
my part, that this selfsame Sermon on the Law
had not proved my public excommunication
from the denomination under the foul brand
of " damnable heresy." But by a great stretch
of charity on the part of two or three old men,
I was saved by a decided majority.

This unfortunate sermon afterwards in-
volved me in a seven years' war with some
members of said Association, and became a
matter of much debate. I found at last, however, that there was a principle at work in the
plotters of said crusade, which Stephen as-
signs as the cause of the misfortunes of
Joseph.

It is, therefore, highly probable to my mind,
that but for the persecution begun on the alleged heresy of this sermon, whether the present reformation had ever been advocated by
me. I have a curious history of many links in

this chain of providential events, yet unwritten and unknown to almost any one living — certainly but to a very few persons — which, as the waves of time roll cn, may yet be interesting to many. It may be gratifying to some, however, at present to be informed that but one of the prime movers of this presumptive movement yet lives; and, alas! he has long since survived his usefulness. I may farther say at present, that I do not think there is a Baptist Association on the continent that would now treat me as did the Redstone Association of that day, which is some evidence to my mind that the Baptists are not so stationary as a few of them would have the world to believe.

But the discourse speaks for itself. It was, indeed, rather an extemporaneous address: for the same spirit that assaulted the discourse when pronounced, and when printed, reversed the resolution of the Association passed on Saturday evening, inviting me to address the audience on Lord's day, and had another person appointed in my place. He providentially was suddenly seized by sickness, and I was unexpectedly called upon in the morning, two hours before the discourse was spoken. A motion was made in the interval, that same day, by the same spirit of jealousy or zealousy, that public opinion should be arrested by having a preacher appointed to inform the congregation on the spot that my " discourse was not Baptist doctrine." One preacher replied, that it might be " Christian doctrine "; for his part, it was new to him, and desired time for examination. I was, therefore, obliged to gather it up from a few notes, and commit it to writing. It was instantly called for to be printed, and after one year's deliberation, at next Association, a party was formed to indict me for heresy on the published discourse. A committee met; resolutions were passed on Friday night. The next day was fixed for my trial; and after asking counsel of Heaven, my sermon was called for, and the suit commenced. I was taken almost by surprise. On my offering immediately to go into an investigation of the matter, it was partially discussed; but on the ground of having no jurisdiction in the case, the Association resolved to dismiss the sermon, without any fuller mark of reprobation, and leave every one to form his own opinion of it. I presume our readers, without any license from an Association, will form their own opinion of it; and, therefore, we submit it to their candid perusal.

A. C.

THE SUBSTANCE OF A SERMON,

Delivered before the Redstone Baptist Association, met on Cross Creek, Brooke County, Va., on the 1st of September, 1816. By Alexander Campbell, one of the Pastors of the Church of Brush Run, Washington County, Pa.

"The law was given by Moses, but grace and truth came by Jesus Christ."—JOHN i, 17.

"The law and the prophets were until John, since that time the kingdom of God is preached, and every man presseth into it."—LUKE xvi, 16.

PREFACE.

To those who have requested the publication of the following discourse, an apology is necessary. Though the substance of the discourse, as delivered, is contained in the following pages, yet, it is not verbatim the same. Indeed, this could not be the case, as the preacher makes but a very sparing use of notes, and on this occasion, had but few. In speaking extempore, or in a great measure so, and to a people who may have but one hearing of a discussion such as the following, many expressions that would be superfluous in a written discourse are in a certain sense necessary. When words are merely pronounced, repetitions are often needful to impress the subject on the mind of the most attentive hearer; but when written, the reader may pause, read again, and thus arrive at the meaning. Some additions, illustrative of the ideas that were presented in speaking, have been made; but as few as could be supposed necessary. Indeed the chief difficulty in enforcing the doctrine contained in the following sheets, either in one spoken or written sermon, consists in the most judicious selection of the copious facts and documents contained in the Divine Word on this subject.

We have to regret that so much appears necessary to be said, in an argumentative way, to the professed Christians of this age, on such a topic. But this is easily accounted for on certain principles. For, in truth, the present popular exhibition of Christianity is a compound of Judaism, Heathen Philosophy, and Christianity; which, like the materials in Nebuchadnezzar's image, does not well cement together.

The only correct and safe course, in this perilous age, is, to take nothing upon trust, but to examine for ourselves, and "to bring all things to the test." "But if any man will be ignorant, let him be ignorant."

As to the style adopted in this discourse, it

is such as we supposed would be adapted to the capacity of those who are chiefly benefited by such discussions. "For their sakes we endeavor to use great plainness of speech." As the doctrines of the gospel are commonly hid from the wise and prudent, and revealed only to babes, the weak and foolish; for their sakes the vail, of what is falsely called eloquence, should be laid aside, and the testimony of God plainly presented to view.

The great question with every man's conscience is, or should be, " What is truth? " Not, Have any of the scribes or rulers of the people believed it? Every man's *eternal all,* as well as his present comfort, depends upon what answer he is able to give to the question Pilate of old (John xviii, 38) proposed to Christ, without waiting for a reply. Such a question can only be satisfactorily answered by an impartial appeal to the oracles of truth—the alone standard of divine truth. To these we appeal. Whatever in this discourse is contrary to them, let it be expunged; what corresponds with them, may the God of truth bless, to those to whom he has given an ear to discern, and a heart to receive it.

ROMANS VIII. 3.

" For what the law could not do, in that it was weak through the flesh, God, sending his own son in the likeness of sinful flesh, and for sin, condemned sin in the flesh."

WORDS are signs of ideas or thoughts. Unless words are understood, ideas or sentiments can neither be communicated nor received. Words, that in themselves are quite intelligible, may become difficult to understand in different connections and circumstances. One of the most important words in our text is of easy signification, and yet, in consequence of its diverse usages and epithets, it is sometimes difficult precisely to ascertain what ideas should be attached to it. It is the term *law*. But by a close investigation of the context, and a general knowledge of the scriptures, every difficulty of this kind may be easily surmounted.

In order to elucidate and enforce the doctrine contained in this verse we shall scrupulously observe the following

METHOD.

1. We shall endeavor to ascertain what ideas we are to attach to the phrase " *the law*,"

in this, and similar portions of the sacred scriptures.

2. Point out those things which *the law* could not accomplish.

3. Demonstrate the reason why *the law* failed to accomplish those objects.

4. Illustrate how God has remedied those relative defects of *the law*.

5. In the last place, deduce such conclusions from these premises, as must obviously and necessarily present themselves to every unbiased and reflecting mind.

In discussing the doctrine contained in our text, we are then, in the first place, to endeavor to ascertain what ideas we are to attach to the terms " *the law*," in this, and similar portions of the sacred scriptures.

The term " *law*," denotes in common usage, " a rule of action." It was used by the Jews, until the time of our Saviour, to distinguish the whole revelation made to the Patriarchs and Prophets, from the traditions and commandments of the rabbis or doctors of the law. Thus the Jews called the Psalms of David *law*. John xii. 34. Referring to the 110th Psalm, they say, " We have heard out of the law that Christ abideth forever." And again, our Saviour calls the Psalms of David *law.* John x. 34. Referring to Psalm lxxxii. 6, he says, " Is it not written in your law, I said ye are gods." Thus when we hear David extolling God's law, we are to understand him as referring to all divine revelation extant in his time. But when the Old Testament scriptures were finished, and divided according to their contents for the use of synagogues, the Jews styled them, the law, the prophets and the psalms. Luke xxiv. 44, Christ says, " All things written in the law of Moses, in the prophets, and in the psalms, concerning me, must be fulfilled."

The addition of the definite article in this instance as well as all others, alters the signification or at least determines it. During the life of Moses, the words " *the law,*" without some explicative addition, were never used. Joshua, Moses' successor, denominates the writings of Moses, " the book of the law "; but never uses the phrase by itself. Nor indeed have we any authentic account of this phrase being used, without some restrictive definition, until the reign of Abijah, 2d Chron. xiv. 4, at which time it was used to denote the whole legal dispensation by Moses. In this way it is used about thirty times in the Old Testament, and as often with such epithets as show that the whole law of Moses is intended.

When the doctrines of the reign of Heaven began to be preached, and to be contrasted in the New Testament with the Mosaic economy, the phrase "*the law,*" became very common, and when used without any distinguishing epithet, or restrictive definition, invariably denoted the whole legal or Mosaic dispensation. In this acceptation it occurs about 150 times in the New Testament. To make myself more intelligible, I would observe that when the terms "*the law*" have such distinguishing properties or restrictive definitions as "the royal law," " the law of faith," " the law of liberty," " the law of Christ," " the law of the spirit of life," etc., it is most obvious the whole Mosaic law or dispensation is not intended. But when we find the phrase " the law," without any such limitations or epithets, as " the law was given by Moses," " the law and the prophets were until John," " if ye be led by the Spirit, ye are not under the law," " ye are not under the law but under grace," etc., we must perceive the whole law of Moses, or legal dispensation, is intended.

I say the *whole* law, or dispensation by
Moses; for in modern times the law of Moses
is divided and classified under three heads, denominated, the moral, ceremonial, and judicial
law. This division of the law being unknown
in the apostolic age, and of course never used
by the Apostles, can serve no valuable purpose,
in obtaining a correct knowledge of the doctrine delivered by the Apostles respecting the
law. You might as well inquire of the Apostles, or consult their writings, to know who the
Supralapsarians or Sublapsarians are, as to inquire of them, what is the moral, ceremonial,
or judicial law. But like many distinctions,
handed down to us from Mystical Babylon,
they bear the mark on their foreheads that cer-
tifies to us their origin is not divine. If this
distinction were harmless, if it did not perplex,
bias, and confound, rather than assist the judgment, in determining the sense of the apostolic
writings, we should let it pass unnoticed; but
justice to the truth requires us to make a remark or two on this division of the law.

The phrase, *the moral law,* includes that part
of the law of Moses, " written and engraved on
two tables of stone," called the ten commandments. Now the word *moral,* according to the

most approved lexicographers, is defined " relating to the practice of men toward each other, as it may be virtuous or criminal, good or bad." The French, from whom we have the term *moral* immediately, and the Romans, from whom we originally received it, used it agreeably to the above definition. Of course, then, a *moral* law, is a law which regulates the conduct of men towards each other. But will the ten commandments answer this definition? No. For Doctors in Divinity tell us, the first table of the Decalogue respects our duty to God; the second our duty to man. Why then call the ten commandments *"the moral law,"* seeing but six of them are moral; that is, relating to our conduct towards men? In modern times, we sometimes distinguish between religion and morality; but while we affirm that religion is one thing, and morality another; and then affirm that the ten commandments are *the moral law* — do we not, in so saying, contradict ourselves? Assuredly the legs of the lame are not equal!

A second objection to denominating the ten precepts, " the moral law," presents itself to the reflecting mind, from the consideration that all morality is not contained in them. When it is said that the ten commandments are "the moral law," does not this definite phrase imply that all morality is contained in them; or, what is the same in effect, that all immorality is prohibited in them? But, is this the fact? Are the immoralities called drunkenness, fornication, polygamy, divorces on trifling accounts, retaliation, etc., prohibited in the ten precepts? This question must be answered in the negative. If it had been asked, is all immorality prohibited in this saying, " thou shalt love thy neighbor as thy self," we would readily answer yes; but it is the so-called moral law we are speaking of. We affirm, then, that the above immoralities are not prohibited in the decalogue, according to the most obvious construction of the words. We are aware that large volumes have been written to show how much is comprehended in the ten precepts. But, methinks, the voluminous works of some learned men on this subject too much resemble the writings of Peter D'Alva, who wrote forty-eight huge folio volumes to explain the mysteries of the conception of the Messiah in the womb of the Virgin Mary! And what shall we think of the genius, who discovered that singing hymns and spiritual songs was prohibited, and the office of the Ruling Elder pointed out, in the second commandment? that dancing and stage plays were prohibited in the seventh; and supporting the clergy enjoined in the eighth! According to this latitude of interpretation, a genius may arise and show us, that law and gospel are contained in the first commandment, and of course all the others are superfluous. But this way of enlarging on the Decalogue defeats the division of the law of Moses, which these Doctors have made. For instance, they tell us that witchcraft is prohibited in the first commandment — incest and sodomy in the seventh. Now they afterwards place these vices, with the laws respecting them, in their judicial law; if then their moral law includes their judicial law, they make a distinction without a difference.

There remains another objection to this division of the law. It sets itself in opposition to the skill of an Apostle, and ultimately deters us from speaking of the ten precepts as he did. Paul, according to the wisdom given unto him, denominated the ten precepts the " ministration of condemnation and of death." 2d Cor. iii. 7, 14. This we call the moral law. Whether *he* or we are to be esteemed the most able ministers of Christ, it remains for you, my friends, to say. Paul having called the ten precepts the ministration of death, next affirms that it was to be done away — and that it was done away. Now the calling the ten precepts " the moral law " is not only a violation of the use of words; is not only inconsistent in itself and contradictory to truth; but greatly obscures the doctrine taught by the Apostle in the 3d chap. 2d Cor., and in similar passages, so as to render it almost, if not altogether, unintelligible to us. To use the same language of the moral law as he used in respect to the ministration of condemnation and death, is shocking to many devout ears. When we say the moral law is done away, the religious world is alarmed; but when we declare the ministration of condemnation is done away, they hear us patiently, not knowing what we mean! To give new names to ancient things, and speak of them according to their ancient names, is perplexing indeed. Suppose, for example, I would call the English law which governed these states when colonies, the Constitution of the United States, and then affirm that the Constitution of the United States is done away, or abolished, who would believe me? But if the people were informed that what *I* called the constitution of these states, was the obsolete British law, they would assent to my statement. Who would not discover that the giving of a wrong name was the sole cause of such a misunderstanding? Hence it is, that modern teachers, by their innovations concerning law, have perplexed the student of the Bible, and caused many a fruitless controversy, as unnecessary as that relating to the mark set on Cain. It does not militate with this statement to grant that some of the precepts of the decalogue have been repromulgated by Jesus Christ, any more than the repromulgation of some of the British laws does not prevent us from affirming that the laws under which the colonies existed are done away to the citizens of the United States. But of this more afterwards.

To what has been said it may be added that the modern division of the law tends very much to perplex any person who wishes to understand the Epistles to the Romans, Galatians and Hebrews; insomuch that while the hearer keeps this distinction in mind, he is continually at a loss to know whether the moral, ceremonial, or judicial law is intended.

Before dismissing this part of the subject we

would observe that there are two principles, commandments, or laws, that are never included in our observations respecting the law of Moses, nor are they ever in holy writ called the law of Moses; these are, " Thou shalt love the Lord thy God with all thy heart, soul, mind, and strength; and thy neighbor as thyself." These, our Great Prophet teaches us, are the basis of the law of Moses, and the Prophets. " On these two commandments hang all the law and the prophets." Indeed the Sinai law, and all Jewish law, is but a modification of them. These are of universal and immutable obligation. Angels and men, good and bad, are forever under them. God, as our Creator, cannot require less; nor can we, as creatures and fellow-creatures, propose or expect less, as the standard of duty and perfection. These are coeval with angels and men. They are engraven with more or less clearness on every human heart. These are the ground work or basis of the law, written in the hearts of heathens, which constitute their conscience, or knowledge of right and wrong. By these their thoughts mutually accuse or else excuse one another. By these they shall be judged, or at least all who have never seen or heard a written law or revelation. But for these principles there had never been either law or gospel. Let it then be remembered that in the scriptures these precepts are considered the basis of all law and prophecy; consequently when we speak of the law of Moses, we do not include these commandments, but that whole modification of them sometimes called the legal dispensation. It must also be observed that the Apostles sometimes speak of the law, when it is obvious that a certain part only is intended. But this, so far from clashing with the preceding observations, fully corroborates them. For if the Apostle refers to any particular part of the law, under the general terms, the law, and speaks of the whole dispensation in the same terms, without any additional definition, then, doubtless, the phrase, the law, denotes the whole legal dispensation, and not any particular law, or new distinction, to which we may affix the words, the law.

2. We shall now attempt to point out those things which the law could not accomplish.

In the first place it could not give righteousness and life. Righteousness and eternal life are inseparably connected. Where the former is not, the latter cannot be enjoyed. Whatever means put us in the possession of the one, puts us in the possession of the other. But this the law could not do. " For if there had been a law given, which could have given life, verily, righteousness should have been by the law." (Gal. iii. 21.) " If righteousness come by the law, then Christ is dead in vain." These testimonies of the Apostle, with the whole scope of divine truth, teach us that no man is justified by the law, that righteousness and eternal life cannot be received through it.

Here we must regret that our translators, by an injudicious supplement, should have made the Apostle apparently contradict himself. I allude to the supplement in the 10th verse of Rom. 7th chap. From the seventh verse of this chapter, the Apostle narrates his experience as a Jew, under the law, and then his experience as a Christian, under the gospel, freed from the law. The scope of the 10th verse, and its context, is to show what the Apostle once thought of the law, and how his mistakes were corrected. If any supplement be necessary in this verse, we apprehend it should be similar to what follows: " And the commandment (which I thought would give me) life, I found (to lead) to death." This doubtless corresponds with the scope of the context, and does not, like the present supplement, clash with Gal. 3d and 21st. Indeed the law, so far from being " ordained to give life," was merely " *added* to the promise of life, till the seed should come to whom the promise was made "—" Moreover the law entered that the offence might abound "—" For by the law was the knowledge of sin." For these reasons we conclude that justification, righteousness and eternal life, cannot by any means be obtained by the law.

2. In the second place, the law could not exhibit the malignity or demerit of sin. It taught those that were under it, that certain actions were sinful — to these sinful actions it gave descriptive names — one is called theft, a second murder, a third adultery. It showed that these actions were offensive to God, hurtful to men, and deserved death. But how extensive their malignity, and vast their demerit, the law could not exhibit. This remained for later times and other means to develop.

3. In the third place, the law could not be a suitable rule of life to mankind in this imperfect state. It could not to all mankind, as it

was given to, and designed only for a part. It was given to the Jewish nation, and to none else. As the inscription on a letter identifies to whom it belongs; as the preamble to a proclamation distinguishes who is addressed; so the preface to the law points out and determines to whom it was given. It points out a people brought from the land of Egypt, and released from the house of bondage, as the subjects of it. To extend it farther than its own preface, is to violate the rules of criticism and propriety. How unjust and improper would it be, to convey the contents of a letter to a person to whom it was not directed — how inconsistent to enjoin the items of a proclamation made by the President of these United States, on the subjects of the French government. As inconsistent would it be to extend the law of Moses beyond the limits of the Jewish nation.— Do we not know with Paul, that what things soever the law saith, it saith to them that are under the law? But even to the Jews it was not the most suitable rule of life. 'Tis universally agreed, that example, as a rule of life, is more influential than precept. Now the whole Mosaic law wanted a model or example of living perfection. The most exemplary characters under the law had their notable imperfections. And as long as polygamy, divorces, slavery, revenge, etc., were winked at under that law, so long must the lives of its best subjects be stained with glaring imperfections. But when we illustrate how God has remedied the defects of the law, the ideas presented in this particular shall be more fully confirmed.

But we hasten to the third thing proposed in our method, which is to demonstrate the reason why the law could not accomplish these objects.

The Apostle in our text briefly informs us, that it was owing to human weakness that the law failed to accomplish these things — " In that it was weak through the flesh." The defects of the law are of a relative kind. It is not in itself weak or sinful — some part of it was holy, just and good — other parts of it were elementary, shadowy, representations of good things to come. But that part of it written and engraven on tables of stone, which was holy, just and good, failed in that it was too high, sublime, and spiritual, to regulate so weak a mortal as fallen man. And even when its oblations and sacrifices were presented, there was something too vast and sublime, for such weak means, such carnal commandments — such beggarly elements — such perishable and insignificant blood, to effect. So that as the Apostle saith, the law made nothing perfect, it merely introduced a better hope. If the law had been faultless, no place should have been found for the gospel. We may then fairly conclude that the spirituality, holiness, justice and goodness of one part of the law, rendered it too high; and the carnal, weak and beggarly elements of another part, rendered it too low; and both together became weak through the flesh. Viewing the law in this light, we can suitably apply the words of the Spirit uttered by Ezek. xx. 25, in relation to its incompetence — "I gave them," says he, "statutes which were not good, and judgments whereby they should not live."

We have now arrived at the 4th head of our discourse, in which we proposed to illustrate the means by which God has remedied the relative defects of the law.

All those defects the Eternal Father remedies, by sending his own Son in the likeness of sinful flesh, and for sin, condemns sin in the flesh. "That the whole righteousness which the law required, might be fulfilled in us, who walk not after the flesh but after the Spirit."

The primary deficiency of the law which we noticed, was, that it could not give righteousness and eternal life. Now, the Son of God, the Only Begotten of the Father, in the likeness of sinful flesh, makes an end of sin, makes reconciliation for iniquity, finishes transgression, brings in an everlasting righteousness, and completes eternal redemption for sinners. He magnifies the law, and makes it honorable. All this he achieves by his obedience unto death. He finished the work which the Father gave him to do; so that in him all believers, all the spiritual seed of Abraham, find righteousness and eternal life; not by legal works or observances, in whole or in part, but through the abundance of grace, and the gift of righteousness, which is by him —" For the gift of God is eternal life through Jesus Christ our Lord." This righteousness, and its concomitant, eternal life, are revealed from faith to faith — the information or report of it comes in the divine word to our ears, and receiving the report of it, or believing the divine testimony concerning it, brings us into the enjoyment of its blessings. Hence it is that Christ is the end of the law for righteousness to every one that believeth. Nor is he on this account the minister of sin — for thus the righteousness, the perfect righteousness of the law, is fulfilled in us who walk not after the flesh, but after the Spirit. Do we then make void the law or destroy the righteousness of it by faith? God forbid: we establish the law.

A second thing which we observed the law could not do, was to give a full exhibition of the demerit of sin. It is acknowledged that the demerit of sin was partially developed in the law, and before the law. Sin was condemned in the deluge, in the confusion of human speech, in turning to ashes the cities of the plain, in the thousands that fell in the wilderness. But these, and a thousand similar monuments beside, fall vastly short of giving a full exhibition of sin in its malignant nature and destructive consequences. But a full discovery of its nature and demerits is given us in the person of Jesus Christ. God condemned sin in him — God spared not his own Son, but delivered him up — It pleased the Lord to bruise him, to pour out his soul an offering for sin. When we view the Son of the Eternal suspended on the cursed tree — when we see him in the garden, and hear his petitions — when we hear him exclaim, "My God, My God, why hast thou forsaken me!" in a word, when we see him expiring in blood, and laid in the tomb, we have a monument of the demerit of sin, which no law could give, which no temporal calamity could exhibit.

We sometimes in the vanity of our minds, talk lightly of the demerit of sin, and irreverently of the atonement. In this age of novelty, it is said, "that the sufferings of Christ were so great as to atone for the sins of worlds on worlds," or at least for the sins of the damned as well as the saved — that "one drop of his blood is sufficient to atone for the sins of the whole world." That is, in other words, the sufferings of Christ so transcended the demerit of the sins of his people, as to be sufficient to save all that shall eternally perish. These assertions are as unreasonable as unscriptural. In our zeal to exalt the merits of the atonement — I say, in the warmth of our passions, and in the fulness of our hearts, let us be cautious lest we impeach the Divine wisdom and prudence. Doubtless, if the merits of his sufferings transcends the demerit of his people's sins, then some of his sufferings were in vain, and some of his merit unrewarded. To avoid this conclusion, some have affirmed that all shall be saved, and none perish, contrary to the express word of God. Indeed, the transition from these inconsistent views of the atonement, to what is called Universalism, is short and easy. But I would humbly propose a few inquiries on this subject. Why do the Evangelists inform us that Christ died so soon after his suspension on the cross? Why so much marvel expressed that he was so soon dead? — so much sooner than the malefactors that were crucified with him? It might be presumed his last words solve these difficulties —"It is finished, and he gave up the ghost." From these and similar premises, it would seem that his life and sufferings were prolonged just so long as was necessary to complete the redemption of his people. We are accustomed, on all subjects that admit of it, to distinguish between quantity and quality. In the common concerns of human intercourse, sometimes the quality of a thing is acceptable when the quantity is not; at other times the quantity is acceptable when the quality is not.

If a thousand slaves were to be redeemed and emancipated by means of gold, the person in whose custody they were could not demand any more precious metal than gold — when one piece of gold was presented to him, he might object to the quantity as deficient, though the quality is unobjectionable. In respect of the means of our redemption, it must be allowed that the sufferings of Christ were they. These sufferings, then, were the sufferings of a divine person — such doubtless was their quality. And a life and sufferings of any other quality, could avail nothing in effecting redemption for transgressors. If but one of Adam's race should be saved, a life and sufferings of such a quality would have been indispensably requisite to accomplish such a deliverance. Again, if more were to have been saved than what will eventually be saved, the quantity and not the quality of his sufferings would have been augmented. The only sentiment respecting the atonement that will bear the test of scripture, truth, or sober reason, is, that the life and sufferings of Christ in quality, and in length or quantity, were such as sufficed to make reconciliation for all the sins of his chosen race; or for all them in every age or nation that shall believe in him. There was nothing deficient, nothing superfluous; else he shall never see of the travail of his soul and be satisfied; which would be the reverse of his Father's promise, and his own expectation. When the life and sufferings of Christ are viewed in this light, the demerit of sin appears in its true colors — all inconsistencies vanish, and all the testimonies of sacred truth, of patriarchs, prophets, and apostles, harmoniously correspond. But if we suppose that the sufferings of Christ transcended the demerit of the sins of " his people," then we have no full exhibition of the demerit of sin. Nor are " his people " under any more obligation of love or gratitude to him than they who eternally perish.

That which remains on this head is to show how the failure of the law in not being a suitable rule of life has been remedied.

We noticed that example is a more powerful teacher than precept. Now Jesus Christ has afforded us an example of human perfection never witnessed before. He gave a living form to every moral and religious precept, which they never before possessed. In this respect he was the distinguished Prophet, to whom Moses and all the inferior prophets referred. In entering on this prophetic office, he taught with a peculiarity unexampled by all his predecessors —" He spake as never man spake." The highest commendation he gave of Moses was that he wrote of him and that he was a faithful servant in Christ's house. From the beginning of his ministry to the end of his life, he claimed the honor of being the only person that could instruct men in the knowledge of God or of his will. He claimed the honor of being the author and finisher of the only perfect form of religion; the Eternal Father attested all his claims and honored all his pretensions. Respecting the ancient rules of life, the law and the prophets, he taught his disciples they had lived their day — he taught them they were given only for a limited time. " The law and the prophets prophesied until John "— then they give place to a greater Prophet, and a more glorious law. Malachi, the last of the ancient prophets, informed Israel that they should strictly observe Moses' law, until a person should come in the spirit and power of Elias. Jesus taught us that John the Baptist was he, and that the law and prophets terminated at his entrance upon his ministry; for since that time the kingdom of God is preached and all men press into it. To attest his character, and to convince the church of his being the great Prophet, to whom all Christians should exclusively hearken as their teacher; to weaken the attachments of his disciples to Moses and the prophets, it pleased God to send down Moses and Elias from heaven; the one the lawgiver, and the other the lawrestorer, to resign their prophetic honors at the feet of the Messiah, in presence of select witnesses. " Jesus took with him Peter, James, and John into a high mountain, and was transfigured before them, and his face did shine as the sun, and his raiment was white as snow, and behold there appeared Moses and Elias talking with him." Peter, enraptured with these heavenly visitants, proposes erecting three tabernacles — one for Christ, one for Moses, and one for Elias. But while he was thus proposing to associate Christ the great Prophet, with Moses and Elias inferior prophets, a bright cloud overshadowed them, and a voice out of the cloud, an indirect reply to Peter's motion —" This is my beloved Son in whom I am well pleased, *hear ye him.*" Thus when these ancient and venerable

prophets were recalled to heaven, Christ alone
is left as the great teacher, to whom, by a commandment from the excellent glory, the throne
of the Eternal, we are obliged to hearken.
That this transaction was significant of the
doctrine above stated, must be manifest, when
we take into view all circumstances. Might it
not be asked, ' Why did not Abel, Abraham,
or Enoch appear on this occasion?' The reason is plain — the disciples of Christ had no
hurtful respect for *them.* Moses and Elias,
the reputed oracles of the Jewish nation, were
the two, and the only two, in respect of whom
this solemn and significant revocation was
needful. The plain language of the whole
occurrence was this — Moses and Elias were
excellent men — they were now glorified in
heaven — they had lived their day — the limited time they were to flourish as teachers of
the will of Heaven was now come to an end.
The morning star had arisen — nay, was
almost set, and the Sun of Righteousness was
arising with salutiferous rays. Let us, then,
walk in the noon-day light — let us hearken
to Jesus as the Prophet and Legislator, Priest
and King. He shall reign over all the ran-
somed race. We find all things whatsoever

the law could not do are accomplished in him, and by him — that in him all Christians might be perfect and complete —" for the law was given by Moses, but grace and truth came by Jesus Christ."

It now remains, in the last place, to deduce such conclusions from the above premises, as must obviously and necessarily present themselves to every candid and reflecting mind.

1st. From what has been said, it follows that there is an essential difference between law and gospel — the Old Testament and the New.* No two words are more distinct in

---

* There are not a few professors of Christianity who suppose themselves under equal obligations to obey Moses or any other Prophet, as Christ and his Apostles. They cannot understand why any part of divine revelation should not be obligatory on a Christian to observe; nor can they see any reason why the New Testament should be preferred to the Old; or why they should not be regulated equally by each. They say, "Is it not all the word of God, and are not all mankind addressed in it?" True, all the holy Prophets spake as they were moved by the Holy Spirit, and men were the objects of their address. It is, however, equally evident that God at sundry times and in diverse manners spake to men, according to a variety of circumstances, which diversified their condition, capacity, and opportunities. Thus he addressed individuals, and classes of individuals, in a way peculiar to themselves. Witness his address to Noah, Abraham, Daniel, Jonah, Paul, and Peter. Witness his addresses to the

their signification than *law* and *gospel.* They
are contradistinguished under various names
in the New Testament. The law is denominated " the letter "; " the ministration of condemnation "; " the ministration of death ";
" the Old Testament or Covenant, and Moses."
The gospel is denominated " the Spirit," " the
ministration of the Spirit," " the ministration
of righteousness," " the New Testament, or
Covenant," " the law of liberty and Christ."
In respect of existence or duration, the former
is denominated " that which is done away "
the latter, " that which remaineth "— the

Patriarchs, the Jews, and the Christians. Again,
men are addressed as magistrates, fathers, masters,
husbands, teachers, with their correlates. Now to
apply to one individual what is said to all individuals
and classes of individuals, would, methinks, appear
egregious folly. And would it not be as absurd to
say, that every man is obliged to practice every duty
and religious precept enjoined in the Bible. Might
we not as reasonably say, that every man must be at
once a Patriarch, a Jew, and a Christian; a magistrate, a subject, a father, a child, a master, a servant,
etc. And, certainly, it is as inconsistent to say,
that Christians should equally regard and obey the
Old and New Testament. All scripture given by
divine inspiration, is profitable for various purposes
in the perfection of saints, when rightly divided, and
not handled deceitfully. But when the above considerations are disregarded, the word of God must
inevitably be perverted. Hence it is that many
preachers deceive themselves and their hearers by

former was faulty, the latter faultless — the former demanded, this bestows righteousness — that gendered bondage, this liberty — that begat bond-slaves, this freemen — the former spake on this wise, "This *do* and thou shalt live "— this says, " Say not what *ye* shall do; the word is nigh thee [that gives life], the word of faith which we preach: if thou believe in thine heart the gospel, thou shalt be saved." The former waxed old, is abolished, and

selecting and applying to themselves and their hearers such portions of sacred truth as belong not to them nor their hearers. Even the Apostles could not apply the words of Christ to themselves or their hearers until they were able to answer a previous question —" Lord, sayest thou this unto *us* or unto *all?* " Nor could the Eunuch understand the Prophet until he knew whether he spoke of himself or of some other man. Yet many preachers and hearers trouble not themselves about such inquiries. If their text is in the Bible, it is no matter where; and if their hearers be men and women, it is no matter whether Jews or Christians, believers or unbelievers. Often have I seen a preacher and his hearers undergo three or four metamorphoses in an hour. First, he is a moral philosopher, inculcating heathen morality; next a Jewish Rabbi, expounding the law; then, a teacher of some Christian precept; and lastly, an ambassador of Christ, negotiating between God and man. The congregation undergo the correlate revolutions: first, they are heathens; next, Jews; anon, Christians; and lastly, treating with the ambassadors for salvation, on what is called the terms of the gospel. Thus, Proteus-like, they are all things in an hour.

vanished away — the latter remains, lives, and is everlasting.

2d. In the second place, we learn from what has been said, that "there is no condemnation to them which are in Christ Jesus." The premises from which the Apostle drew this conclusion are the same with those stated to you in this discourse. "Sin," says the Apostle, "shall not have dominion over you; for ye are not under the law, but under grace." In the 6th and 7th chapters to the Romans, the Apostle taught them that "they were not under the law"— that "they were freed from it"—"dead to it"—"delivered from it." In the 8th chapter, 1st verse, he draws the above conclusion. What a pity that modern teachers should have *added to* and *clogged* the words of inspiration by such unauthorized sentences as the following: "Ye are not under the law" *as a covenant of works, but as a rule of life.* Who ever read one word of the "covenant of works" in the Bible, or of the Jewish law being a rule of life to the disciples of Christ? Of these you hear no more from the Bible than of the "Solemn League" or "St. Giles' Day." Yet how conspicuous are these and kindred phrases in the theological discussions of these last three hundred years! But leaving such phrases to those who are better skilled in the use of them, and have more leisure to expound them, we shall briefly notice the reason commonly assigned for proposing the law as a rule of life to Christians. "If Christians are taught," say they, "that they are delivered from the law, under it in no sense, that they are dead to it, will not they be led to live rather a licentious life, live as they list; and will not the non-professing world, hearing that *they* are not under the law of Moses, become more wicked, more immoral and profane?" Such is the chief of all the objections made against the doctrine inculcated respecting the abolition of the Jewish law, in respect of Christians, and also as this doctrine respects the Gentile or Heathen world. We shrink not from a fair and full investigation of this subject. Truth being the only allowed object of all our inquiries, and the sole object of every Christian's inquiry, we should patiently hear all objections — coolly and dispassionately hear, examine, and weigh all arguments pro and con.

That the first part of this objection is very natural, has been very often made, and strongly urged against the doctrine we advocate, we cheerfully acknowledge. As this objection was made against the Apostle's doctrine concerning the law, it affords a strong probability, at least, that our views on this subject correspond with his. We shall then hear how he stated and refuted it. Rom. vi. 15. " What then? Shall we sin because we are not under the law, but under grace?" Here he admits the objection, and in his answer incontestably shows that Christians are not under the law in any sense. If they were in any sense, now was the time to say, " We are not under the law in some sense, or under a certain part of it; but in one sense we are under it, as a rule of life." We say the Apostle was here called upon, and in a certain sense bound, to say something like what our modern teachers say, if it had been warrantable. But he admits the doctrine and states the objection, leaving the doctrine unequivocally established. He guards the doctrine against a licentious tendency thus —" God forbid!" " How shall we that are dead to sin, live any longer therein?" and in the subsequent verses shows the utter impossibility of any servant of God, or true Christian, so abusing the doctrine we

have stated. Now whether the ancient way
of guarding the New Testament, or Gospel,
against the charges of Antinomianism or a
licentious tendency, or the modern way is best,
methinks is easily decided amongst true disciples. Not so easy, however, amongst learned
Rabbis and Doctors of the Law.

But, query — Is the law of Moses a rule of
life of Christians? An advocate of the popular doctrine replies, "Not all of it." Query
again —"What part of it?" "The ten commandments." Are these a rule of life to Christians? "Yes." Should not, then, Christians
sanctify the seventh day? "No." Why so!
"Because Christ has not enjoined it." Oh!
then, the law or ten commandments is not a
rule of life to Christians any further than it
is enjoined by Christ; so that reading the
precepts in Moses' words, or hearing him utter
them, does not oblige us to observe them: it
is only what Christ says we must observe.
So that an advocate for the popular doctrine,
when closely pressed, cannot maintain his
ground. Let no man say we have proposed
and answered the above queries as we pleased.
If any other answers can be given by the advocates themselves than we have given, let them

do it. But it is highly problematical whether telling Christians that they are under the law will repress a licentious spirit. True Christians do not need it, as we have seen: "how shall they that are dead to sin, live any longer therein?" And dare we tell professing Christians, as such, that the law, as a rule of life, is a condemning law? If not, then what tendency will the mere affirmation that they are under a law as a rule of life which cannot condemn them, have to deter them from living as the list. Upon the whole, the *old way* of guarding against immorality and licentiousness amongst Christians will, we apprehend, be found the most consistent and efficacious. And he that has tried the old way and the new, will doubtless say, as was said of old, "No man also having drunk old wine, straightway desireth new; for he saith the old is better." And, indeed, every attempt to guard the New Testament, or the Gospel, by extrinsic means, against an immoral or licentious tendency, bears too strong a resemblance to the policy of a certain preacher in Norway or Lapland, who told his hearers that "hell was a place of infinite and incessant cold." When asked by an acquaintance from the south of Europe why he perverted the scriptures, he replied, " if he told his hearers in that cold climate that hell was a place of excessive heat, he verily thought they would take no pains to avoid going there."

But as to the licentious tendency this doctrine we inculcate is supposed to have upon the non-professing or unbelieving world, it appears rather imaginary than real. It must, however, in the first instance be ascertained whether the Gentiles, not professing Christianity, were ever supposed or addressed by the Apostle sent to the Gentiles, as being under the law of Moses. We have under the second head of our discourse particularly demonstrated that the Gentiles were never under the law, either before or after their conversion. To what has been said on this subject we would add a sentence or two. It was prophesied of the Gentiles that they should be without law until Christ came. Isai. xlii. 4. " And the isles shall *wait* for *his* law." The chief glory which exalted the Jews above the Gentiles, which the Jews boasted of to the Gentiles, was, that *to them " pertained* the adoption, the covenants, and *the giving of the law."* They exclusively claimed the law as their own. And

why will not we let them have it, seeing him
whose law the Gentiles waited for is come,
and has given us a more glorious law. Whatever was excellent in their law our Legislator
has re-promulgated. But shall we say that we
are under the law as a rule of our Christian
life because some of its sublimest moral and
religious precepts have been re-promulgated
by him who would not suffer one title of it to
pass till he fulfilled it? As well might we
affirm that the British law which governed
these states when colonies is the rule of our
political life; because some of the most excellent laws of that code have been re-enacted by
our legislators. Paul, the Apostle to the Gentiles, plainly acknowledged in his addresses to
them, that they were without law, aliens from
the commonwealth of Israel, having no hope,
etc. And of them he said that "when the
Gentiles, which have not the law, do by nature
the things contained in the law, these *having
not the law,* are a law unto themselves." But,
in so saying, does *he* or do *we* excuse their
sins or lead them to suppose that they are
thereby less obnoxious to the wrath to come?
By no means. For we testify that even natural
conscience accuses them of sin or wrong in

their thoughts, words, and actions, according to its knowledge. And consequently " as many as have sinned without law, shall also perish without law." In so testifying, do we cherish a licentious spirit? By no means. For there stand a thousand monuments in this present world, independent of Jewish law, on which is inscribed these words, " For the wrath of God is revealed from heaven against all ungodliness and unrighteousness of men." But one thing demands our observation, that the Apostle sent by Heaven to preach to the Gentiles, in accusing them of sins of the deepest dye, and of the most malignant nature, dishonorable to God and destructive to themselves, never accuses them of any sin which the light of nature itself would not point out, or natural conscience testify to be wrong. Hence it is that in the long black catalogue of sins preferred against the Gentiles, is never to be found the crime of Sabbath-breaking, or of transgressing any of the peculiarities of Judaism. And now what is the difference between an ancient Greek and a modern American or European who disbelieves the gospel? Under what law is the latter, under which the former was not? Was the former a sinner and chargeable in the sight of God, as well as the latter? Yes. Would not natural conscience according to its means of knowing right and wrong, or the work of the law written in the heart, condemn the unbelieving Roman as well as the unbelieving American? Most assuredly. And what is the difference? Not that the latter is under any law that the former was not under, but the means of discerning right and wrong in the latter are far superior to the former, and consequently their overthrow or ruin will be more severe. In point of law or obligation there is no difference between the unbelieving American and the rudest barbarian; though the former is polished with science, morals, etc., like the ancient Greeks and Romans, and the latter remains an uncultivated savage. They will be judged and condemned by the same law which condemned the Roman who died 1900 years ago. And the condemnation of the latter shall be more tolerable than the former, not by a milder law, but because his knowledge of right and wrong was much inferior to the former; and having heard the gospel of salvation and disbelieved it, he adds to his natural corruption and accumulated guilt the sin of making

God a liar, and preferring darkness to light, because he believed not the testimony of God. This is the sole difference in respect of condemnation between the Indian and the most accomplished citizen. From these few remarks it will appear, we trust, obvious to every person who has an ear to distinguish truth from falsehood, that there is no condemnation to them which are in Christ Jesus — that they are under no law that can condemn them — that *he* who was made under the law is become the end of the law for righteousness to them — that being dead to sin, they should live no longer therein — that there is no necessity, but a glaring impropriety in teaching the law as a rule of life to Christians — that all arguments in favor of it are founded on human opinion, and a mistaken view of the tendency of the gospel and Christian dispensation — that all objections against the doctrine we have stated, as licentious in its tendency, are totally groundless. "For the grace of God that bringeth salvation teacheth us that denying ungodliness and worldly lusts, we should live soberly, righteously, and godly in this present world. Looking for that blessed hope, the glorious appearing of the great God, even our

Savious Jesus Christ; who gave himself for us that he might redeem us from all iniquity, and purify unto himself a peculiar people, *zealous of good works."*

3d. In the third place, we conclude from the above premises, that there is no necessity for preaching the law in order to prepare men for receiving the gospel.

This conclusion perfectly corresponds with the commission given by our Lord to the Apostles, and with their practice under that commission. " Go," saith he, " into all the world, and preach the gospel unto every creature." " Teach the disciples to observe all things whatsoever I command you." Thus they were authorized to preach the gospel, not the *law,* to every creature. Thus they were constituted ministers of the New Testament, not of the Old. Now the sacred history, called the Acts of the Apostles, affords us the most satisfactory information on the method the Apostles preached under this commission; which, with the epistolary part of the New Testament, affords us the only successful, warrantable, and acceptable method of preaching and teaching. In the Acts of the Apostles, we see the Apostles and first preachers paid the most scrupulous regard to the instructions they received from the great Prophet. They go forth into all nations proclaiming the gospel to every creature; but not one word of law-preaching in the whole of it. We have the substance of eight or ten sermons delivered by Paul and Peter to Jews and Gentiles, in the Acts of the Apostles, and not one precedent of preaching the law to prepare their hearers, whether Jews or Gentiles, for the reception of the gospel.

This conclusion corresponds, in the next place, with the nature of the kingdom of heaven or Christian church, and with the means by which it is to be built and preserved in the world. The Christian dispensation is called " the ministration of the Spirit," and accordingly everything in the salvation of the church is accomplished by the immediate energy of the Spirit. Jesus Christ taught his disciples that the testimony concerning himself was that only which the Spirit would use in converting such of the human family as should be saved. He was not to speak of himself, but what he knew of Christ. Now he was to convince the world of sin, of righteousness, and of judgment; not by applying the law of Moses, but the facts concerning Christ, to the consciences of the people. The Spirit accompanying the words which the Apostles preached, would convince the world of sin; not by the ten precepts, but because they believed not on him — of righteousness, because *he* went to the Father — and of judgment, because the prince of this world was judged by him. So that Christ, and not law, was the Alpha and Omega of their sermons; and this the Spirit made effectual to the salvation of thousands. Three thousand were convinced of sin, of righteousness, and of judgment, in this precise way of hearing of Christ, on the day of Pentecost; and we read of many afterwards. Indeed, we repeat it again, in the whole history of primitive preaching, we have not one example of preaching the law as preparatory to the preaching or reception of the gospel.

This conclusion corresponds, in the third place, with the fitness of things.* That men

---

* Indeed we have yet to learn what advantage can accrue from preaching the so-called "moral law," to prepare sinners for the gospel. In the nature and fitness of things it cannot prepare or dispose the mind to a belief of the gospel. The Apostle teaches us that "the law worketh wrath."

must be convinced of sin by some means, prior to a welcome reception of saving truth, is generally acknowledged. Now as the gospel dispensation is the most perfect revelation of salvation, it must be supposed that it possesses the best means of accomplishing every thing connected with the salvation of its subjects. It must, of course, possess the best means of convincing of sin. This truth, however, does not depend on mere supposition. The fact that the Holy Spirit makes an exclusive use

This is inevitably its effect on every mind which does not believe the gospel. It irritates and excites the natural enmity of the mind against God. A clear exhibition of the divine character in the law, apart from the gospel, tends more to alienate than to reconcile the mind to God. When a preacher of the law has labored to show his hearers the immaculate holiness, the inflexible justice, the inviolate truth, and consuming jealousy of Jehovah, manifested in the fiery law, supposing the gospel kept out of view, he has rather incapacitated and disqualified their minds from crediting the gospel or testimony of the condescension, love, mercy, and grace of the eternal Father to mankind. How opposite is the divine wisdom to the wisdom of many modern scribes and teachers of the law! They preach first the law to natural fallen man, then the gospel. But He, who seeth not as man seeth, preached first the gospel to a fallen man, and afterwards added the law, because of transgressions, till the seed should come. Eternal life was promised through the seed, and the law added till the seed come.

of it in convincing of sin, is a striking demonstration of its superior excellence for that purpose. But independent of these considerations, it must be confessed that the gospel or testimony concerning Christ affords the fullest proof of divine justice and indignation against sin — it presents the clearest view of the demerit of sin, and of all divine perfections terrible to sinners — it exhibits the most alarming picture of human guilt and wretchedness that ever was given, and on these ac-

Nothing can be more inconsistent than the conduct of the law preachers. When they have echoed the thunders of Mount Sinai in the ears of their hearers almost to drive them to despair, and to produce what they call "legal repentance," then they begin to pull down the work of their own hands by demonstrating the inefficacy, unprofitableness, and danger of legal repentance. Might they not as well at once imitate the Apostles and primitive preachers — preach the gospel, which, when received, produces repentance not to be repented of? Might they not preach Christ crucified, in whom is manifested the wrath and judgment of God against sin; and his condescending love, mercy, and grace to the sinner. Might they not, knowing the terror of the Lord, persuade men by the persuasives of the doctrine of reconciliation, rather than to increase their enmity, awaken their suspicions, and work wrath in their minds, by an unlawful use of the law? But in order to this, their minds must be revolutionized; they must take up a cross which they at present refuse: and what is difficult indeed, they must unlearn what they have themselves taught others.

counts is of all means the most suitable to convince of sin. It was already observed that the eternal Father condemned sin in the person of his Son more fully than it ever was, or could be, condemned in any other way. Suppose, for illustration, a king put to death his only son, in the most painful and ignominious way, for a crime against the government: would not this fact be the best means of convincing his subjects of the evil of crime, and of the king's detestation of it? Would not this fact be better than a thousand lectures upon the excellency of the law and the sanctions of it? But every similitude of this kind falls infinitely short of affording a resemblance of the eternal Father not sparing his Sole Delight when sin was but imputed to him. Having seen that this conclusion corresponds with the commission given by the Redeemer to his Apostles — with their practice under that commission — with the nature of his kingdom, and with the fitness of things; one would suppose that no objection could be preferred against it. But what doctrine of divine truth is it, against which objections numerous indeed, and strongly urged, and by men who profess to be zealous for the truth, have not been made! Is it the doctrine of sovereign, free, and abundant grace? No. Is it the doctrine of the natural sinfulness and corruption of all men. No, no. Against these, many objections, yea, very many, are urged. We must not suppose, then, that this doctrine we now maintain shall be free from objections. We shall, then, attend to some of those objections which have been made, or which we anticipate may be made, against this conclusion.

It may, perhaps, be objected that there are some expressions in the apostolic epistles, which imply that the law was necessary to convince of sin, as pre-requisite to a welcome reception of the gospel: such as " by the law *is* the knowledge of sin "—" for without the law sin *was* dead." There is no authority from the original for varying the supplements in these two clauses. If it corresponds with the context or with the analogy of faith, to supply *was* in the last clause, it doubtless corresponds as well in the first clause. But we lay no stress on the one or the other; for before Christ came all knowledge of sin *was* by the law; and " the law entered that the offence might abound." For the law was added to the promise of life, because of transgression, till the seed should come to whom the promise was made. Now we would suppose that when the *Seed* is come, and the time expired for which the law was added, it is superfluous to annex it to the gospel, for the same reason it was annexed to the promise made to Abraham. And although it should be allowed that Christians derive knowledge of sin from the law, it does not follow that it is the best means of communicating this knowledge — that Christians are dependent on it for this purpose — nor that it should be preached to unbelievers to prepare them for receiving the gospel.

The seventh chapter to the Romans contains the fullest illustration of the once excellence and utility of the law, that is to be found in all the New Testament; and as this chapter will doubtless be the stronghold of our opponents, we shall make a remark or two on the contents of it.

In the first place, then, let it be remembered that in the fourteenth verse of the preceding chapter, the Apostle boldly affirms that Christians are not under the law. To the conclusion of the sixth chapter he refutes an objection made to his assertion in the fourteenth verse. In the first six verses of the seventh chapter he repeats his assertion, and uses an apt similitude to illustrate it. Having, then, demonstrated that Christians are not under the law, in the seventh verse of the seventh chapter he states an objection which had been made, or he anticipated would be made, against his doctrine — "If Christians are not under the law, if they are dead to it, if they are delivered from it, is it not a sinful thing?" "Is the law sin, then?" This objection against the nature of the law, the Apostle removes in the next six verses by showing the utility of the law in himself as a Jew, under that law; and concludes that the law is holy, just, and good. To the end of the chapter the Apostle gives an account of his experience as a Christian freed from the law, and thus manifests the excellency of his new mind or nature by its correspondence to the holiness of the law; so that he most effectually removes the objection made against the law as being sin, and at the same time establishes the fact that Christians *are delivered from it.* Such evidently is the scope of the latter part of the sixth and all of the seventh chapter. We cannot dismiss this chapter without observing first, that the law, or that part of the law which the Apostle here speaks of, is what modern teachers call " the moral law." If so, then Christians are not under it; for the law which the Apostle affirms Christians are delivered from in the sixth verse, in the seventh verse he shows it is not sin; and the law which he shows is not sin, he demonstrates to be holy, just, and good. So that here, as well as in the third chapter of his second epistle to the Corinthians, Christians are expressly said to be delivered from the so-called moral law; and that it is abolished or done away in respect of them. We must remark again, that before any thing said in this chapter respecting the utility or excellence of the law, can be urged as a precedent for what we condemn — namely, preaching the law as preparatory to the gospel, or a law work as preparatory to genuine conversion, it must be shown that the Apostle gave this account of his experience under the law as preparative to his conversion. Otherwise no objection can be made from anything in this chapter to the conclusion before stated. But this cannot be; for the account we have of his conversion flatly contradicts such a sup-

position. Previous to his conversion he was
a very devout man in his own way —"touching the righteousness which was in the law
he was blameless." See the account he gives of
himself, Phil. iii. 4, 5, compared with Rom.
vii. 7, 12; Acts xxii. 1; xxiii. 1; from which
we learn that he was taught according to the
most perfect manner of the law, and was a
Pharisee of the strictest kind; had clear ideas
of sin and righteousness; and, externally considered, was blameless and lived in all good
conscience until the day of his conversion.
But it was not the law, it was not a new discovery of its spirituality, but a discovery of
Christ exalted, that convinced him of sin, of
righteousness, and of judgment; and instan-
taneously converted him. So that nothing in
his previous life or attainments, nothing of his
experience as a Jew, nothing of his knowledge
of sin or of righteousness by the law previous
to his conversion, can be urged in support of
preaching the law or a law work to unbelievers, to prepare their mind for a welcome reception of the truth.

When we shall have mentioned a favorite
text of the law preachers, and considered it,
we shall have done with objections of this sort.

It is Galatians iii. 24. We shall cite from the 23d verse. "Before faith [Christ] came we were kept under the law, shut up unto the faith which should afterwards be revealed. Wherefore the law was our schoolmaster *to bring us* to Christ, that we might be justified by faith. But after that faith [Christ] is come, we are no longer under a schoolmaster." Methinks it looks rather like an insult to the understanding of any person skilled in the use of words, to offer a refutation of the use that is frequently made of the 24th verse. But let the censure rest upon them who render it needful. Every smatterer in Greek knows that the 24th verse might read thus: "The law was our schoolmaster until Christ" came; and this reading unquestionably corresponds with the context. Now is it not most obvious that instead of countenancing law-preaching, this text and context condemn it? The scope of it is to show that whatever use the law served as a schoolmaster previous to Christ, it no longer serves that use. And now that Christ is come, we are no longer under it. We see, then, that this conclusion not only corresponds with the commission to the Apostles; with the nature of Christ's kingdom; with the apostolic preaching; and with the fitness of things: but that no valid objection can be presented against it, from any thing in the apostolic epistles.

Some, notwithstanding the scriptural plainness of this doctrine, may urge their own experience as contrary to it. It would, however, be as safe for Christians to make divine truth a test of their experience, and not their experience a test of divine truth. Some individuals have been awakened by the appearance of the Aurora Borealis, by an earthquake, by a thunderstorm, by a dream, by sickness, etc. How inconsistent for one of these to affirm from his own experience, that others must be awakened in the same way! How incompatible with truth for others to preach such occurrences as preliminary to saving conversion!

But the difference between ancient and modern conversions is so striking as to merit an observation or two. Now that the law is commonly preached to prepare men for Christ, it must be expected that modern conversions will be very systematic, and lingering in all. While preachers will not condescend to proclaim the glad tidings until they have driven their hearers almost to despair by the thunders of Mount Sinai — while they keep them in anxious suspense for a time, whether the wounds of conviction are deep enough; whether their sense of guilt is sufficiently acute; whether their desires are sufficiently keen; whether their fears are sufficiently strong; in short, whether the law has had its full effect upon them: I say, when this is the case, conversion work must go on slow; and so it is not rare to find some in a way of being converted for years; and, indeed, it is generally a work of many months. It would be well, however, if, after all, it were commonly genuine. Contrast these conversions with those of which we read in the Acts of the Apostles, and what a contrast! There we read of many converted in a day, who yesterday were as ignorant of law and gospel as the modern Hindoos or Birmans. To account for this we have only to consider and compare the different sorts of preaching and means by which those and these are effected.

But some may yet inquire, are unbelievers under no law or obligation by which conviction may be communicated to their minds? Or they may ask, in other words, How does the testimony of Christ take hold of them? And why do they welcome the gospel? We have already shown that there is a law written on every human heart, which is the foundation of both law and prophets, under which both angels and men exist; whose obligation is universal and eternal. It is inscribed more or less distinctly on every heathen's heart. It is sometimes called the law of nature, but more correctly called by the Apostle, *conscience*. This natural conscience, or sense of right and wrong, which all men possess in different degrees, according to a variety of circumstances, but all in some degree, is that in them which God addresses. This natural conscience is fitted to hear the voice of God, as exactly as the ear is fitted to hear sounds. This renders the savage inexcusable. For the invisible things of God, even his eternal power and godhead, are manifested to his conscience in the natural world. Now God addresses conscience in those whom he brings to himself in a variety of ways. Sometimes even where his word is come, he speaks by awful events to the consciences of men. In this way he awakens inquiries that lead to the saving truth. Witness the jailor and his house, of whom we

read in the Acts of the Apostles. God spake
to his conscience by an earthquake, and put
an inquiry in his mouth, that was answered to
his salvation and that of his house. That
which fits the savage to hear God's voice in
the natural world, fits him, or the man of
civilization, to hear his voice in the gospel,
when it is sent to them in power.

Are we to preach this law of nature, then,
some will inquire; or are we to show men that
they possess this natural conscience, previous
to a proclamation of the glad tidings? I would
answer this question by proposing another.
Am I to tell a man he has an ear, and explain
to him the use of it, before I condescend to
speak to him? One answer suits both inquiries. We should consider the circumstances
of any people before we address them. Do we
address Jews? Let us address them as the
Apostles did. Persuade them out of their own
law that Jesus is the Messiah. Do we address
professed Christians? Let us imitate the apostolic addresses in the epistles. Do we preach
to Barbarians? Let us address them as Paul
preached to the Lycaonians. Speak to their
consciences. Do we preach to polished infidels
or idolaters? Let us speak to them as Paul

spake to the Athenians. Speak to their consciences.

4th. A fourth conclusion which is deducible from the above premises is, that all arguments and motives, drawn from the law or Old Testament, to urge the disciples of Christ to baptize their infants; to pay tithes to their teachers; to observe holy days or religious fasts, as preparatory to the observance of the Lord's supper; to sanctify the seventh day; to enter into national covenants; to establish any form of religion by civil law: and all reasons and motives borrowed from the Jewish law, to excite the disciples of Christ to a compliance with or an imitation of Jewish customs, are inconclusive, repugnant to Christianity, and fall ineffectual to the ground; not being enjoined or countenanced by the authority of Jesus Christ.

5th. In the last place we are taught from all that has been said, to venerate in the highest degree the Lord Jesus Christ; to receive Him as the Great Prophet, of whom Moses in the law, and all the prophets did write. To receive him as the Lord our righteousness, and to pay the most punctilious regard to all his precepts and ordinances. " If we continue in his word, then are we his disciples indeed, and we shall know the truth, and the truth shall make us free — if the Son shall make us free, we shall be free indeed."

It is remarkable how strong our attachments are to Moses as a teacher; though Moses taught us to look for a greater prophet than he, and to hearken *to him!* It is strange that three surprising incidents in the history of Moses would not arrest our attention and direct us to Christ. With all his moral excellence, unfeigned piety, and legislative dignity, he fell short of Canaan. So all who cleave to him will come short of the heavenly rest! His mortal remains, and his only, the Almighty buried in secret; and yet we will not suffer his ashes to rest in peace! He came down from heaven to give place to the Messiah, to lay down his commission at his feet; and we will not accept it! Strange infatuation!

If Moses was faithful in Christ's house as a servant, shall not Christ be faithful as a son over his own house? Let us as his disciples believe all he teaches, and practice all he enjoins in religion and morality; let us walk in all his commandments and ordinances; and inquire individually, What lack I yet! If we

are then deficient, let us say, with the Jews
who disowned him, " We are Moses' disciples,
but as for this fellow, we know not whence
he is." But let all remember that if he that
despised Moses' law, died without mercy, of
how much sorer punishment, suppose ye, shall
he be thought worthy, who despised Christ as
a teacher! His commandments are not grievous to his disciples — his yoke is easy, and his
burden is light.

Let every one that nameth the name of
Christ depart from all iniquity. Let us walk
worthy of him. Let us take heed lest by our
conduct we should represent Christ as the
minister of sin. Let us not walk after the
flesh but after the Spirit; and then we shall
show that the righteousness of the law is fulfilled in us. Then shall no occasion be given
to the adversary to speak reproachfully. And
if any should still urge the stale charge of
Antinomianism, or affirm that we lived in sin
that grace might abound; did evil that good
might come; or made void the law through
faith; let us put to silence the ignorance of
foolish men, by adorning the doctrine we profess with a blameless conduct. Let us not
merely rebut such insinuations with a — God

forbid! but evince, how shall we that are dead to sin, live any longer therein.

May he that hath the key of David, who openeth and no man shutteth, and shutteth and none can open, open your hearts to receive the truth in the love of it, and incline you to walk in the light of it, and then ye shall know that the ways thereof are pleasantness, and all the paths thereof are peace! AMEN.

Isaac Errett

E VERY great movement must have an adequate name and personality accounting for its origin. And for its progressive unfolding, it equally requires adequate names and personalities.

In this latter class, no name and personality stand out with greater prominence and are significant of more superb vital service than those of Isaac Errett.

Standing as a junior with the fathers in the most intimate relations and supplementing their labors with his princely abilities as an orator, and with his almost unmatched style as a writer, he was early identified with the historical undertakings of the Disciples of Christ, and was unapproachable as the natural successor of the greatness of the first generation. Stepping into the places of high service and influence as the greatest severally vacated them, he was easily able to serve the cause as he found it, with utmost efficiency and with increasing acceptance and honor to the end of his life. Isaac Errett was born in New York City, January 2, 1820. His father, Henry Errett, was officially identified with the New

York City Church, about the time of the issue
of the Declaration and Address of Thomas
this early day of the Reformation, Henry
Campbell and his son Alexander. Like the
strong men in many isolated communities in
Errett stood forth in New York and Danbury,
Connecticut, and probably elsewhere in the
East, contending, as the Campbells and Stone
and others were, for the abolition of the evils
of sectarianism by the Bible method of Christian Union.

Isaac Errett grew up in a family of six
sons, who in early life sustained the great
loss of losing their father. At ten years
of age his school career terminated, and two
years later he became a member of the church
in Pittsburg. At the age of twenty he married
Miss Harriet Reeder, who was a woman of
uncommon mental and moral endowments, and
gave her best with singular devotion to him
and the children of their union, who perpetuate his name onward. After serving the
church in Pittsburg for several years, he was
called to the pastorate of the church in New
Lisbon, Ohio, in the year 1844. Here he
preached for five years and gave increasing
evidence of the possession of those rare powers

which ever afterwards marked and distinguished him as the chief master of assemblies, both state and national.

His pastorates after this time were at North Bloomfield and Warren, Ohio. In Michigan he did a great constructive work during his residence of ten years at Detroit and Muir, and for a part of that period he was corresponding secretary of the American Christian Missionary Society.

Returning to Ohio, in 1866, he settled in Cleveland, where he was to enter the greater field of his life work, for which all earlier days had prepared him.

Up to this time the great paper of the brotherhood, since the time of Alexander Campbell, was the *American Christian Review.* That paper, with Benjamin Franklin as its editor, was predominant in our field of journalism. Suffice it to say, that everywhere a great need was felt for a journal of superior culture and the broadest conception of the unsearchable riches of Christ. A paper that would deal with all living questions in the spirit of patient inquiry and blameless toleration, and that would discover the truth in its fulness, maintain it without bigotry and rancor, and yet with true, knightly courage and dignity, and guide its readers into the best fields of literature and revelation. Such a journal was needed and desired by a growing constituency throughout our brotherhood.

Such brethren as the Phillips brothers (four of them), of New Castle, Pennsylvania; James A. Garfield, of Hiram, Ohio; J. P. Robison, of Cleveland; and Harrison Jones, of Ohio, with G. W. N. Yost, of Cory, Pennsylvania, all foremost men of eastern Ohio and western Pennsylvania, were the founders of the *Christian Standard,* the warm personal friends of Isaac Errett, who regarded him as the man to fulfill the highest and best hopes of the people of their day.

The Phillips brothers were the rich men of this corporation, and a working fund of $25,-000 was raised and spent and sunk in the attempt to place the new venture upon a financial basis. The paper passed through some trying vicissitudes, but after several years, through the commanding ability and influence of its able editor, reached the period of success.

During these years, when Isaac Errett was the great editor of the *Christian Standard,* he grew into kingly power and rose to that sta-

tion of eminence among his brethren for which
he was providentially designed as surely as
his compeers of the preceding years. He filled
a place as unique as theirs, and the service he
rendered to the rising generation of preachers
and the thoughtful men and women who ate at
the feast and drank of the pure wine which he
weekly provided, has molded the church of the
present age with his own large, liberal and
sweet spirit, and established them in intelligent
and devout loyalty to the Word of God and
the scintillant life of Jesus the Christ.

If Alexander Campbell was mighty in the
service of the truth, as its demands were known
in his day, the later demands of the truth as
they were presented to his lieutenant and val-
iant successor, were courageously confronted
and appreciated with singular vividness and
delicacy of discernment and fully and grandly
answer for the instruction and encouragement
of the people, young and old, of to-day who
look with unspeakable affection and respect
upon him who stands between them and the
earliest fathers in Israel, like Saul, among his
brethren, and yet with his hand of love and
comradeship upon all their heads to the youngest. The church of to-day cherishes Isaac

Errett with grateful pride and enthusiasm, and is exceedingly moved by his words and works and the Christly spirit pervading all his famous personality, so that while it accords large and tender hospitality to the man who in this day best keeps the garrison of the truth after his princely fashion, the brotherhood will never let one of their grandest historic names lose its power among them.

ISAAC ERRETT.

Our Position

CHAPTER I.

In answer to numerous inquiries and requests, we deem it advisable to set forth, in brief and direct terms, a statement of the position and aims of the Disciples in their plea for a restoration of primitive Christianity. It will not require large space, as our design is not to argue, but simply to state our position. Under three heads we can easily present all that needs to be said:

I. *That in which we agree with the parties known as evangelical.*

II. *That in which we disagree with them all.*

III. *That in which we differ from some, but not from all of them.*

First, then, let us state that much is held by us in common with the parties known as evangelical; nay, there is scarcely anything recognized by them as essential or vital, that is not as truly and as firmly held by us as by them.

*A brief statement of the plea for a return to the Gospel and the Church of Apostolic Times, urged by the people known as Disciples of Christ. By Isaac Errett, Editor of the "Christian Standard."

We are one with them in holding to and advocating the following items of doctrine:

1. The divine inspiration of the Holy Scriptrues of the Old and New Testaments.

2. The revelation of God, especially in the New Testament, in the tri-personality of Father, Son and Holy Spirit.

3. The alone-sufficiency and all-sufficiency of the Bible, as a revelation of the divine character and will, and of the gospel of grace by which we are saved; and as a rule of faith and practice.

4. The divine excellency and worthiness of Jesus as the Son of God; his perfect humanity as the Son of man; and his official authority and glory as the Christ — the Anointed Prophet, Priest and King, who is to instruct us in the way of life, redeem us from sin and death, and reign in and over us as the rightful Sovereign of our being and Disposer of our destiny. We accept therefore, in good faith, the supernatural religion presented to us in the New Testament, embracing in its revelations,

(1) The incarnation of the Logos — the eternal Word of God — in the person of Jesus of Nazareth.

(2) The life and teachings of this divinely

anointed Lord and Savior, as the highest and completest unfolding of the divine character and purposes, as they relate to our sinful and perishing race, and as an end of controversy touching all questions of salvation, duty and destiny.

(3) The death of Jesus as a sin-offering, bringing us redemption through his blood, even the forgiveness of sins.

(4) His resurrection from the dead, abolishing death and bringing life and immortality clearly to light.

(5) His ascension to heaven, and glorification in the heavens, where he ever liveth the Mediator between God and Man — our great High Priest to intercede for his people; and our King, to rule until his foes are all subdued and all the sublime purposes of his mediatorial reign are accomplished.

(6) His supreme authority as Lord of all.

5. The personal and perpetual mission of the Holy Spirit, to convict the world of sin, righteousness and judgment, and to dwell in believers as their Comforter, Strengthener and Sanctifier.

6. The alienation of the race from God, and their entire dependence on the truth, mercy

and grace of God, as manifested in Jesus, the Christ, and revealed and confirmed to us by the Holy Spirit in the gospel, for regeneration, sanctification, adoption and life eternal.

7. The necessity of faith and repentance in order to the enjoyment of salvation here, and of a life of obedience in order to the attainment of everlasting life.

8. The perpetuity of Baptism and the Lord's Supper, as divine ordinances, through all ages to the end of time.

9. The obligation to observe the first day of the week as the Lord's day, in commemoration of the death and resurrection of Jesus Christ, by acts of worship such as the New Testament teaches, and by spiritual culture such as befits this memorial day.

10. The church of Christ, a divine institution, composed of such as, by faith and baptism, have openly confessed the name of Christ; with its appointed rulers, ministers and services, for the edification of Christians and the conversion of the world.

11. The necessity of righteousness, benevolence and holiness on the part of professed Christians, alike in view of their own final sal-

vation, and of their mission to turn the world to God.

12. The fullness and freeness of the salvation offered in the gospel to all who accept it on the terms proposed.

13. The final punishment of the ungodly by an everlasting destruction from the presence of the Lord and from the glory of his power.

These thirteen items certainly present a broad basis of agreement in conceptions of divine truth which may rightfully be termed catholic. It would be passing strange that a people who hold heartily and unequivocally to these fundamental truths and principles should be regarded as unevangelical, did we not know the inveterateness of religious prejudice, and the inevitable lot of all who plead for religious reformation to be misunderstood and misrepresented. Time, however, wears away this prejudice, and as our opponents come out from the mist into a clearer view of the positions they have attacked, they try to believe that we have changed wonderfully from what we were, and are now *almost* orthodox! They can thus gracefully concede to us the present possession of truth without seeming to confess their own error in having misapprehended us in the past. But we pause not for controversy on this. It is not of so much importance to know who was right or wrong in the past, as to be sure who is right *now*. We have simply to say that we stand now where we have always stood on the points above stated. We presume not to say that no one among us has ever said anything subversive of any of the truths or principles we have enunciated; for in the controversies of fifty years it must be expected that some unripe or erratic minds would give utterance to some halftruths which are necessarily errors. Nor do we say that even the soundest advocates of our plea have not sometimes been tempted to indulge in partial views and ungrounded utterances. They must have been more than men had they escaped the operation of those laws, of mind which govern it in breaking away from extremes, or when absorbed in the discussion of particular points of doctrine. The inevitable result is ultraism in a greater or less degree. But we do say, and wish to be emphatic in saying, that from the first day that this plea for a return to primitive Christianity began, until this day, there has been no doubt and no controversy among its leading advocates, and none among the mass of its intelligent adherents, on the thirteen points we have named. Not only have they accepted these teachings, but they have been ready at all times to advocate and defend them against all unbelievers and errorists.

We do not say this with any view to crave a place among the evangelicals. For ourselves we look with increasing indifference on conventional standards of orthodoxy. It is a small thing to be judged by men. We desire to be found standing in the ranks of the honest advocates of truth, whether that advocacy lift us to the approval of the multitude, or sink us under the heaviest ban of the popular will. The frowns of men can not kill, their smiles can not save. Better to share the cross of Jesus than the approval of the multitudes that condemned him. Let us not, therefore, be misunderstood. We write not to soften any angularities in our plea, or to win it favor by any compromise with the opposition. But where there is agreement, for the truth's sake we desire to be understood; and at a time when there is so much need for the united sympathy and labors of all who love our Lord Jesus Christ, it is important to avoid all false issues and urge no differences that are not real and serious.

We shall be better understood when we state the points of difference.

CHAPTER II.

Particulars in which we Differ from all Others, and in which consequently the Peculiarities of our Plea most Strikingly Appear.

1. While agreeing as to the divine *inspiration* of the Old and New Testaments, we differ on the question of their equal binding *authority* on Christians. With us, the Old Testament was of authority with *Jews,* the New Testament is *now* of authority with *Christians.* We accept the Old Testament as true and as essential to a proper understanding of the New, and as containing many invaluable lessons in righteousness and holiness which are of equal preciousness under all dispensations, but as a *book of authority* to teach *us* what *we* are to do, the New Testament alone, as embodying the teachings of Christ and his apostles, is our standard.

2. While accepting fully and unequivocally the Scripture statements concerning what is usually called the trinity of persons in the Godhead, we repudiate alike the philosophical and theological speculations of Trinitarians and

297

Unitarians, and all unauthorized forms of speech on a question which transcends human reason, and on which it becomes us to speak " in words which the Holy Spirit teaches." Seeing how many needless and ruinous strifes have been kindled among sincere believers by attempts to define the indefinable, and to make tests of fellowship of human forms of speech which lack divine authority, we have determined to eschew all such mischievous speculations and arbitrary terms of fellowship, and to insist only on the " form of sound words," given to us in the Scriptures concerning the Father, the Son, and the Holy Spirit.

3. While agreeing that the Bible furnishes an all-sufficient revelation of the Divine will, and a perfect rule of faith and practice, we disagree practically in this; *We act consistently with this principle,* and repudiate all human *authoritative* creeds. We object not to publishing, for information, what we believe and practice, in whole or in part, as circumstances may demand, with the reasons therefor. But we stoutly refuse to accept of any such statement as authoritative, or as a test of fellowship, since Jesus Christ alone is Lord of the conscience, and His word alone can rightfully bind

us. What He has revealed and enjoined, either personally or by His apostles, we acknowledge as binding; where He has not bound us, we are free; and we insist on standing fast in the liberty wherewith Christ hath made us free, carefully guarding against all perversions of said liberty into means or occasions of strife.

4. With us, the Divinity and Christhood of Jesus is more than a mere item of doctrine — it is the central truth of the Christian system, and in an important sense the Creed of Christianity. It is the one fundamental truth which we are jealously careful to guard against all compromise. To persuade men to trust and love and obey a Divine Savior, is the one great end for which we labor in preaching the gospel; assured that if men are right about Christ, Christ will bring them right about everything else. We therefore preach Jesus Christ and him crucified. We demand no other faith, in order to baptism and church membership, than the faith of the heart in Jesus as the Christ, the Son of the living God; nor have we any term or bond of fellowship but faith in this Divine Redeemer and obedience to Him. All who trust in the Son of God and obey Him, are our brethren, however wrong they may be about

anything else; and those who do not trust in this Divine Savior for salvation and obey his commandments, are not our brethren, however intelligent and excellent they may be in all beside. Faith in the unequivocal testimonies concerning Jesus — his incarnation, life, teachings, sufferings, death for sin, resurrection, exaltation, and Divine sovereignty and priesthood; and obedience to the plain commands he has given us; are with us, therefore, the basis and bond of Christian fellowship. In judgments merely inferential, we reach conclusions as nearly unanimous as we can; and where we fail, exercise forbearance, in the confidence that God will lead us into final agreement. In matters of expediency, where we are left free to follow our own best judgment, we allow the majority to rule. In matters of opinion — that is, matters touching which the Bible is either silent or so obscure in its revelations as not to admit of definite conclusions — we allow the largest liberty, so long as none judges his brother, or insists on forcing his own opinion on others, or on making them an occasion of strife.

5. While heartily recognizing the perpetual agency of the Holy Spirit in the work of con-

version — or, to use a broader term, regeneration — we repudiate all theories of spiritual
operations and all theories of the Divine and
human natures which logically rule out the
word of God as the instrument of regeneration
and conversion, or which make the sinner pas-
sive and helpless, regarding regeneration as a
miracle, and leading men to seek the evidence
of acceptance with God in supernatural tokens
or special revelations, rather than in the
definite and unchangeable testimonies and
promises of the gospel. We require assent to
no theory of regeneration, or of spiritual influence; but insist that men shall hear, believe,
repent, and obey the gospel — assured that if
we are faithful to God's requirements on the
human side of things, He will ever be true to
himself and to us in accomplishing what is
needful on the *Divine* side. Our business is
to preach the gospel, and plead with sinners to
be reconciled to God; asking God, while we
plant and water, to give the increase. We care
little for the logic of any theory of regeneration, if we may but persuade sinners to believe,
repent, and obey.

6. While agreeing with all the evangelical
in the necessity of faith and repentance, we

differ in this: We submit *no other tests* but faith and repentance, in admitting persons to baptism and church membership. We present to them no Articles of Faith other than the one article concerning the Divinity and Christhood of Jesus; we demand no narration of a religious experience other than is expressed in a voluntary confession of faith in Jesus; we demand no probation to determine their fitness to come into the church; but instantly, on their voluntary confession of the Christ, and avowed desire to leave their sins and serve the Lord Christ, unless there are good reasons to doubt their sincerity, they are accepted and baptized, in the name of the Lord Jesus, and *into* the name of the Father, the Son and the Holy Spirit. They are thus wedded to *Christ,* and not to a set of doctrines or to a party.

7. We not only acknowledge the perpetuity of baptism, but insist on its meaning, according to the Divine testimonies: " He that believeth and is baptized *shall be saved."* Repent and be baptized, every one of you, in the name of Jesus Christ, *for the remission of sins,* and you shall receive the gift of the Holy Spirit." We therefore teach the believing penitent to seek,

through baptism, the divine assurance of the forgiveness of sins, and that gift of the Holy Spirit which the Lord has promised to them that obey him. Thus, in a hearty and scriptural surrender to the authority of the Lord Jesus, and not in dreams, visions, or revelations, are we to seek for that assurance of pardon and that evidence of sonship to which the gospel points us.

The Lord's Supper, too, holds a different place with us from that which is usually allowed to it. We invest it not with the awfulness of a sacrament, but regard it as a sweet and precious feast of holy memories, designed to quicken our love of Christ and cement the ties of our common brotherhood. We therefore observe it as part of our regular worship, every Lord's day, and hold it a solemn, but joyful and refreshing feast of love, in which all the disciples of our Lord should feel it to be a great privilege to unite. " Sacred to the memory of our Lord and Savior Jesus Christ," is written on this simple and solemn family feast in the Lord's house.

8. The *Lord's* day — not the Jewish Sabbath — is a New Testament observance, which

is not governed by statute, but by apostolic example and the devotion of loyal and loving hearts.

9. *The Church of Christ* — not sects — is a Divine institution. We do not recognize sects, with sectarian names and symbols and terms of fellowship, as *branches* of the Church of Christ, but as unscriptural and anti-scriptural, and therefore to be abandoned for the one Church of God which the New Testament reveals. That God has a people among these sects, we believe; we call on them to come out from all party organizations, to renounce all party names and party tests, and seek only for *Christian* union and fellowship according to apostolic teaching. Moreover, while we recognize the seeming necessity for various denominational movements in the past, in the confusions growing out of the great apostasy, we believe that the time has now fully come to urge the evils and mischiefs of the sect spirit and sect life, and to insist on the abandonment of sects and a return to the unity of spirit and union and co-operation that marked the churches of the New Testament. We therefore urge the word of God against human creeds; faith in Christ against

faith in systems of theology; obedience to Christ rather than obedience to church authority; the Church of Christ in place of sects; the promises of the Gospel instead of dreams, visions and marvelous experiences as evidences of pardon; Christian character in place of orthodoxy in doctrine, as the bond of union; and associations for co-operation in good works instead of associations to settle questions of faith and discipline.

It will thus be seen that our differential character is found not in the advocacy of new doctrines or practices, but in rejecting that which has been added to the original simple faith and practice of the Church of God. Could all return to this, it would not only end many unhappy strifes and unite forces now scattered and wasted, but would revive the spirituality and enthusiasm of the early church; as we should no longer need, as in the weakness of sectism, to cater to the world's fashions and follies to maintain a precarious existence, Zion could again put on her beautiful garments and shine in the light of God, and go out in resistless strength to the conquest of the world. To this end, we are not asking any to cast away their confidence in Christ, or to part with aught that is Divine; but to cast away that which is human, and be one in clinging to the Divine. Is it not reasonable? Is it not just? Is it not absolutely necessary, to enable the people of God to do the work of God?

CHAPTER III.

Points in which we Agree with Some, but not with All.

1. In regard to immersion, we agree with all immersionists. The meaning of the Greek term; its literal and metaphorical uses in the New Testament; the incidental allusions to the primitive practice; the testimonies of the ecclesiastical history as to the primitive practice; the testimonies of the leading reformers, such as Luther, Calvin and Wesley, and the admission of a host of lexicographers and critics by practice affusionists, but compelled as scholars to admit the truth as to the meaning of the word and the primitive practice; these have led us to the definite and fixed conclusion that immersion is that which Christ ordained. Moreover, as an effort to restore the primitive *catholicity* of the church is a prominent feature in our work, we could not be blind to the fact that immersion is catholic, while sprinkling and pouring are not. The advocates of affusion, while stoutly contending for it as scriptural, nevertheless admit that immersion also is baptism. Some do this

on philological and historical grounds; but even the extremest advocates of affusion, while disputing the philological and historical arguments for immersion, still admit that it will be accepted, on the ground that the *form* is not essential to the *thing*. So it happily turns out that, by various routes, we can all reach an agreement respecting immersion as baptism, and respecting immersion *only*. We therefore hold to that which bears the stamp of catholicity, and reject that which lacks it.

2. Touching the *subjects* of baptism, we are also in accord with Baptist bodies, and at variance with Pedobaptists. Here, again, are we on catholic ground. There is no controversy as to the baptism of *believers* in Christ; the dispute relates entirely to the baptism of such as do not or can not believe. Infant baptism lacks the stamp of catholicity; believers' baptism has it.

3. As to the *design* of baptism, we part company with Baptists, and find ourselves more at home on the other side of the house; yet we can not say that our position is just the same with that of any of them. Baptists say that they baptize believers *because they are forgiven,* and they insist that they shall have

the evidence of pardon before they are baptized. But the language used in the Scriptures declaring what baptism is for, is so plain and unequivocal, that the great majority of Protestants, as well as Roman Catholics, admit it in their creeds to be, in some sense, for the remission of sins. The latter, however, and many of the former, attach to it the idea of regeneration, and insist that in baptism regeneration by the Holy Spirit is actually conferred. Even the Westminster Confession squints strongly in this direction, albeit its professed adherents of the present time attempt to explain away its meaning. We are as far from this ritualistic extreme as from the anti-ritualism into which the Baptists have been driven. With us, regeneration must be so far accomplished before baptism that the subject is changed in heart, and in faith and penitence must have yielded up his heart to Christ — otherwise baptism is nothing but an empty form. But *forgiveness* is something distinct from *regeneration*. Forgiveness is an act of the Sovereign — not a change of the sinner's heart; and while it is extended in view of the sinner's faith and repentance, it needs to be offered in a sensible and tangible form, such that the sinner can seize it and appropriate it with unmistakable definiteness. In baptism he *appropriates God's promise of forgiveness,* relying on the divine testimonies: " He that believeth and is baptized shall be saved." " Repent and be baptized, every one of you, in the name of Jesus Christ, for the remission of sins, and ye shall receive the gift of the Holy Spirit." He thus lays hold of the promise of Christ and appropriates it as his own. He does not *merit* it, nor *procure* it, nor *earn* it, in being baptized, but he *appropriates* what the mercy of God has provided and offered in the gospel. We therefore teach all who are baptized that if they bring to their baptism a heart that renounces sin and implicitly trusts the power of Christ to save, they should rely on the Savior's own promise — " He that believeth and is baptized shall be saved."

4. In regard to the beginning of the Church of Christ, there is a general agreement among leading theologians and ecclesiastical historians to date it from the day of Pentecost succeeding the resurrection of our Lord from the dead; but this is not the view accepted by any of the religious parties as such. Pedobaptist churches

generally teach that the Jewish and Christian churches are the same, the latter being merely an enlargement and improvement of the former. Baptists confine the Church of Christ to the New Testament, but many of them are disposed to date it from the ministry of John the Baptist. With us, it is held that the first church of Christ was planted at Jerusalem on the day of Pentecost referred to, of which we have an account in Acts ii.; that the Jewish institution, with the authority of Moses as lawgiver, passed away when Jesus bowed his head on the cross and said, " It is finished "; that the lawgiver, the covenant, the laws, the subjects, the promises of the new institution, are different from those of the old; and that from that time onward the terms of salvation, the rules of life, the laws of association, the spirit and genius of religion, are to be learned from Christ and his apostles, and only from Moses and the prophets as these point to those and prepare the way for them. The Bible, therefore, takes on very simple and easy divisions. The Old Testament is introductory to the New. The four Gospels present the knowledge of Jesus, and the evidences on which our faith in this Divine Redeemer should rest. The Acts of the Apostles show how the gospel of salvation was preached and accepted — how sinners were made Christians, and were associated in churches as a spiritual brotherhood. The Epistles were addressed to *Christians,* furnishing a knowledge of Christian duties, rights, privileges, dangers, trials, and hopes, and preparing them unto all good works. The Apocalypse is supposed to deal with the fortunes and final destiny of the Church of Christ.

5. In point of church government we agree in the main with Congregationalists and Baptists; but not altogether. The distinction of *clergy* and *laity* is not known among us. All Christians are royal priests to God. Preachers, teachers and rulers are not a caste in any sense. For the sake of order and efficiency we have elders or bishops, deacons, and evangelists; yet in the absence of these our members are taught to meet, to keep the ordinances and encourage each other to love and to good works, and may baptize, administer the Lord's Supper, or do whatever needs to be done to promote their own growth and the salvation of sinners. Nevertheless, as soon as suitable gifts are developed, persons are chosen to act as elders and deacons, and to serve in any other

ministry the church may need. The details of government and discipline are left largely with the elders, they being responsible to the church for their doings.

We have no ecclesiastical courts, properly speaking, outside the individual churches; but it is becoming somewhat general now to refer difficult and unmanageable cases to a committee mutually agreed on by the parties concerned — their decision to be final. Our District, State and National assemblies are not for the discussion or decision of matters of doctrine or discipline, but for co-operation in good works.

6. As it relates to the question of *union*, when this movement began, the plea for the union of Christians was peculiar to it. The growth of that sentiment, however, has been so extensive of late years, that it can no longer be said to be peculiar. One important feature of it remains with us as peculiar still. While there is a general confession of the evils of sectarianism, and a general desire to see a union of Christians brought about, no definite basis or plan of union has been presented. Here all are yet groping in the dark, and most are dreaming of attaining to a desirable *unity* with-

out actual union — thus preserving their pet denominationalisms, and at the same time flattering themselves that they are getting away from sectarianism. We have, however, from the first, presented and practiced a definite plan of union. The presentation of this feature of our plea belongs to another chapter.

CHAPTER IV.

In closing this sketch, we wish to fix attention on our attitude to the Union question. There is now a very general acknowledgment of the evils and mischiefs, if not of the actual sin, of sectism. It has not always been so. When this plea for the restoration of primitive Christianity was first made, its prominent features was a denunciation of the folly and wickedness of sects among Christians, and a plea for a restoration of the catholicity of the apostolic churches. This plea had but few sympathizers then. It was met with suspicion, with doubt, with indifference, with cavil and disputation, with storms of denunciation as an undesirable and utopian scheme. There was a united opposition on the part of the denominations generally, because they saw that this doctrine struck at their very roots as denominations, and was directly antagonistical to everything that belonged to mere sect life. Within the last few years, however, a great revolution of public sentiment on this question has been developed. It is no longer necessary to argue, in most com-

munities, the *desirableness* of Christian union;
that is freely conceded — nay, more, it is elo-
quently and ably argued and illustrated by
hundreds of tongues and pens in the various
evangelical denominations.

Still it must be confessed that the union
movement is in a nebulous state. The subject
is handled by most writers in a gingerly way.
There is painful evidence that the best minds
are cramped by their ecclesiastical associations,
and are groping after some scheme of union or
of sect-affiliation, that will avoid the sacrifice
of party idols, and enable sectarians to secure
the blessings of a broader fellowship by pay-
ing down but part of the price.

The different phases of this movement may
be thus stated:

1. The Broad-church phase. This, if we
understand it — as it reveals itself in England
— would leave all questions, even the most
vital and fundamental, such as the Divinity of
Christ and the inspiration of the Scriptures,
open to all who, in a general way, will assent
to the requirements of the Church of England,
or any other State establishment, subject to
whatever mental reservations may be necessary
in each case; and thus have a National Church

ample enough and liberal enough in its provisions to meet the wants of all. While we
see much to admire in the lives and labors of
the gifted men who lend the influence of their
powerful names to this scheme, we confess to
a sort of disgust whenever we stop to think of
the sordid *policy* which leads such men to cling
to an establishment with whose doctrines and
ritual they have no sympathy which would not
die out in a day if their *livings* were not in question. It is, to say the very least, ungenerous to
seek to subvert the very life of the institution
on which they are dependent for the bread
which gives strength to the hand that strikes
the deadly blow at a mother's heart. It is not
to the credit of the rationalism of this age that
so many of its advocates are meanly subsisting
and fattening on the spoils of a religion which
they disbelieve, and allowing themselves to
cling mercenarily to a false position. The
cause of God has nothing to hope for from a
source so meanly selfish and corrupt.

2. The *Unity* phase — the abstract union-
ists. These regard *unity* as desirable, but
union as impracticable. They advocate a
moonshiny sentimentalism of catholicity of
spirit which they are well assured cannot

be realized in *life*. They propose that the sects
remain undisturbed in their separate organizations and interests, and merely be put on their
best behavior toward each other. The highest
aim they propose is a *confederation* of sects
for general purposes, in which all agree, leaving all local and rival interests and opposing
doctrines to adjust themselves as best they can.
How far short this is of any scriptural model,
need not be argued here. We can not forbear
quoting the language of Isaiah, as finding a
not inapt significance here, albeit the original
design of it was altogether different: " Say
ye not, a confederacy, to all to whom this people shall say, a confederacy; neither fear ye
their fear, nor be afraid. Sanctify the Lord of
hosts himself, and let him be your fear, and let
him be your dread."

3. The Organic Union phase. This finds
varied expression. With some, it is simply the
organic union of kindred sects on common denominational ground, or the making of one
big sect out of several smaller ones; leaving
further attempts to the subduing influences of
time. With others, it is an earnest and avowed
attempt to unite the leading evangelical denominations in one, simmering down their

creeds into a few articles of concentrated orthodoxy such as all orthodox Christians can accept, and such as will serve at the same time to fence out all who are suspected of a want of orthodoxy.

From one point of view, we sympathize with all these phases of the union movement. We are glad of every utterance which tends to break down sectarian barriers; of every step which condemns the folly and weakness of denominationalism. It is perhaps needful that just such preparatory measures should be adopted to open the way for something better. It is in the right direction, and the public mind, once led as far away from the old denominational landmarks as these leaders will conduct it, can not well go back into the sectarian fastnesses of the past. but as a *consummation*, none of these proposed measures is devoutly to be wished. " They do but skin and film the ulcerous place." They fail to reach the roots of the disease, and they timidly propose no more than a temporary expedient.

Let us now state the doctrine of Christian Union as taught and practiced by us.

1. It frankly avows not only the folly, but the *sin* of sectarianism, and teaches that, just

as any other sin, it must be abandoned. It proposes no compromise whatever with denominationalism, but insists that party names, party creeds, and party organizations, being in direct contravention of the teachings of Christ, must be forsaken. It distinguishes between sects going away from the Church of God into Babylon, and sects coming back from Babylon, seeking to find the Church of God. With these latter it has much sympathy, and offers for their imperfect yet important and salutary movements in reformation, many apologies. Still it insists that the return from Babylon to Jerusalem is incomplete so long as rival and jarring sects are found in place of the one catholic apostolical church of primitive times.

2. It insists that unity and union are practicable; that in the first age of the church our Lord and his apostles did establish one grand spiritual brotherhood, and did embrace in it men of all classes and nationalities, however diverse or antagonistical their sentiments, tastes, and habits may previously have been; and that the Christless condition of society at that time presented much greater obstacles in the way of such a union than any that are

found now among the professed followers of Christ. The difficulties should therefore be manfully met in the face and overcome.

3. It proposes simply a return, "in letter and in spirit, in principle and in practice," to the original basis of doctrine and of fellowship. Seeking after this it finds,

(1) That all who put their trust in Jesus as the Christ, the Son of God, and for His sake left their sins and renounced all other lordships, were at once accepted as worthy to enter this fellowship. *Faith in the Divine Lord and Savior was the one essential condition of entrance.* None could enter without faith — infant membership was therefore impossible. None who had faith could be refused admission — no other test was allowed but that of faith in and submission to Jesus, the Christ. We therefore proclaim, in opposition to all big and little creeds of Christendom, *that the original creed has but one article of faith in it, namely:* That Jesus is the Christ, the Son of God. All doctrinal tests but this must be abandoned.

(2) That all such believers were admitted into this fellowship by baptism, upon the authority of Jesus Christ, into the name of the

Father, and of the Son, and of the Holy Spirit. We have said in a former chapter, that there ought to be no stumbling here if there is indeed a desire for union; since all admit that immersion is baptism, and nothing else is admitted by all. It can only be the stubbornness of the sect-spirit that prevents union in that which all can accept. The only real difficulty here in the way relates to those who have received pouring or sprinkling in adult years, and have conscientious scruples about repeating, as they would regard it, an obedience already rendered. These, however, are exceptional cases, and would soon adjust themselves if it were once settled that nothing should hereafter be practiced but that which all agree to be sufficient.

(3) That among these baptized believers there was no spiritual caste — no distinction of clergy and laity; but all were brethren, and none was to be called Master or Father. The order of the church must harmonize with this. Nothing must be insisted on as of Divine authority, or be made a test of fellowship, for which there is not a *thus saith the Lord,* in express precept or approved precedent.

4. In all matters where there is no express

precept or precedent, the law of love should lead us to that which will promote edification and peace.

a. In matters merely inferential, unanimity is to be sought, but not forced.

b. In matters merely prudential, the majority should rule, care being had, however, not to transcend the limits of expediency by contravening any Divine precept; and regard always being had to the prejudices and the welfare of all.

c. Where Christ has left us free, no man has a right to judge his brother. The largest liberty is here allowed, limited only by the spirit of the apostolic teaching: " If meat cause my brother to stumble, I will eat no meat while the world stands."

Such is, in brief, what we propose as a basis of union. We have no desire for mere organic union any faster than a supreme love for Christ leads to unity of spirit, and prepares men for the voluntary sacrifice of all but Christ.

We have no faith in the practicability of uniting sects on any merely sectarian basis, however liberal. It can not be Christian union unless it is union in Christ — in that which Christ enjoins, neither less nor more. The present unwillingness, with all the prevalent union sentiment, to abandon sectarian names and interests, proves how unavailing all attempts at a union of parties, as such, must prove. We do not, therefore, propose the union of sects; but call on all the people of God in the various sects to come out from them and unite in the faith and practice of the New Testament. We propose in this way to subvert sectarianism — calling the lovers of Jesus out from sects, and leavening those who refuse to come with the doctrine of the New Testament until they too shall be ready to give up the sect for Christ.

CHAPTER V.

Objections to Our Position.

There are some objections to the plan of union on which we are acting which deserve attention.

I. That while we profess to repudiate everything sectarian and to advocate only that which is catholic, we do practically establish a sectarian test — admitting none but those who accept our *interpretation* of the meaning of baptism. An affusionist is not allowed to have his own interpretation, but must bend to ours.

This, if true, would be a serious objection. But, in truth, it is not, with us a question of *interpretation* at all, but of *translation*. We propose to unite with all believers in Christ Jesus *on the word of God* — to accept what it teaches, and do what it commands. As the word of God was not originally spoken or written in English, we must have it translated in such words as will faithfully convey " the mind of the Spirit." What we insist on is, that *baptizo* is not fairly represented in English by pour, or sprinkle, or wash, but by dip, plunge, immerse.

This being so, a faithful translation leaves no necessity for party interpretation as to the thing required to be done. We repeat, therefore, that we impose our interpretations on none; we simply ask that the word of God shall be faithfully translated. The question is philological.

If it be said that there is doubt as to the proper translation of the original term, we reply: No more doubt than can be raised over any other term that men may choose to dispute about; not so much as may be plausibly urged against many other leading terms in the New Testament, and none that can present a serious obstacle to union, provided the *spirit* of union is in the ascendant. This will be apparent in the light of the following statements:

1. All the lexicographers of note give dip, plunge, immerse as the literal meaning of *baptizo*.

2. Ecclesiastical history clearly proves not only that immersion was the primitive practice, but that it continued to be the general practice for over twelve centuries.

3. The Greek Church has always practiced it, and continues to practice it to this day.

4. The Western or Roman Catholic Church

freely admits that the original practice was immersion, and does not pretend to base its present practice on the meaning of the word, or the authority of Scripture; but claims that the *church* has authority to change the ordinances. Both affusion and infant membership are maintained on the ground of *tradition,* by the Roman Catholics, it being freely admitted that they are not to be proved from Scripture alone.

5. Affusion and infant membership obtained a footing among the Reformers *as an inheritance from Rome,* and not on the ground of Scripture authority. They imported them from Babylon as the fruits of their religious training, found themselves in possession of them, and were put to it to find some authority from Scripture to justify them.

6. Luther, Calvin and Wesley all admitted frankly that immersion was the apostolic practice. Calvin justified sprinkling, on the ground that the church had the authority to modify the *form* somewhat, retaining the *substance;* but, he added, " the word baptize signifies to immerse, and *it is certain* that immersion was the practice of the ancient church."

7. Immersion was that which the rubric of the Church of England required at the time the

Presbyterians came into power in England and formed their Directory for Public Worship. They changed it so as to read that sprinkling was not only lawful, but sufficient, and carried it by the casting vote of the Moderator — no one presuming to deny the lawfulness of immersion.

When we add to these considerations what we said in a previous number — that immersion can be accepted by all as valid baptism — it will be seen that we are neither attempting to impose an interpretation on any, nor to tyrannize over the conscience of any. We insist on that which the word of God enjoins, and which all can accept without a sacrifice of conscience.

II. It is objected that the creed which we submit is too broad — it will let in heretics of various stripes, and the church will soon be loaded down with an intolerable burden of error.

To this we reply:

1. That the question to be met is not, is this good policy? or, What will come of it? — let such inquiries be put when nothing more sacred than mere expedients are in question — but, Was this the primitive practice? Is this

what the apostles taught? It is beyond controversy that, in preaching the gospel and turning
sinners to Christ, the apostles knew and were
determined to know nothing but Jesus Christ
and him crucified. It is equally certain that
they received sinners to baptism upon their
avowed faith in Jesus as the Christ, the Son
of the living God. It is not impious on our
part to question the wisdom of heaven's ar-
rangements and ordinations? How dare we
impose either doctrinal or practical barriers
where they imposed none?

2. The human inventions by which it
has been sought to keep out heresy and heretics
have not been successful. They have made
more heresy than they have cured or prevented,
and, in place of preventing the increase of
parties, have been the fruitful sources of division. If sometimes they have kept out those
who were unsound in the faith, have they not
also kept out many of whom God would accept — kept them out because they could not
accept the traditions of men? The practical
result of human tests is not seen in a united
nor yet in a pure church, but quite the reverse.

3. If men are ever persuaded to love and
trust in Jesus as a Divine Savior, they can

readily be brought right about all else. The normal development of the love of Christ as the sovereign power in the soul will conquer and annihilate errors much more readily than the assertion of merely human authority or a formal assent to church dogmas. The early converts to Christianity had many errors in possession, as is evident from the New Testament history; but the apostles evidently trusted that they would outgrow them as rapidly as they advanced in the knowledge and love of Christ. They therefore left them undisturbed in their possession *so long as they did not seek to impose them on others,* or so long as these errors did not subvert their faith in Christ. The apostles were jealous of everything that would move men's confidence away from Christ or supplant His authority; they were tolerant in all beside. Let us here quote the words of another:

" Put Christ in your temple, and whatever ought not to be there will depart at his bidding. Is your congregation disturbed by the presence of birds or beasts that defile it? Open the door to Him and give Him full possession, for He alone has the power to drive them out. Is the temple of your heart infested with the beasts of selfishness, which show their presence in the works of the flesh? You can not expel them by your will alone. Put Christ in your temple.

" There are yet those who are vainly trying to cleanse the temple of its falsehood by a scourge of small cords of doctrine spun out of their own brain. There are those who are seeking to expel from churches organs, festivals, etc., by the force of their own personal menaces; and there are not wanting those who are seeking to cleanse their own lives by their low keeping in their own strength. Put Christ in your temples, and whatever ought not to be there He will drive out."*

4. It may be possible to unite men in the faith and love of Jesus, the Christ, so as to have one common brotherhood in all the earth, inspired by a common faith, and hope, and love; but it is not possible to establish a catholic brotherhood on any creed of man's devising. The really catholic church — the only true Catholic Church — that of the first and second centuries — had no human creed.

III. It is objected that there is much beyond the Divinity of Christ taught in the Scriptures,

---

* Alex Procter.

and that, if Christians are to be properly instructed, the truths of the Bible must be faithfully taught.

Answer:

1. Unquestionably. These truths, disciples are to learn *after they come into the church,* but they are not tests by which they are admitted. Teachers should fully instruct the church in all that the Bible teaches, but the members are not bound to receive such instructions any further than they see them established by Scripture testimony. But if the teacher becomes heretical — what then? Let the church cease to employ him in that capacity.

2. There is a class of speculative questions which can not enter into the teaching of the pulpit, and which can have no proper place in a creed, because they are not questions of *faith,* but of *opinion;* yet their discussion may, in a philosophical point of view, be valuable. All these questions should be relegated to the schools of philosophy where they belong, and there should be freely discussed without danger of ecclesiastical interference.

IV. It is objected that the clashing interests of the various systems of church government will not allow of union.

Our Position

We reply that when the spirit of Christ shall become superior to the pride of sect, no question of church polity will be allowed to divide Christians. Church government does not stand among the terms of salvation. If, as is generally argued, the Scriptures give us no definite form of church government, and therefore these various forms have grown up according to necessity, it is evident they can *come down* again according to a new necessity; and he is not acting as a Christian who would allow anything not Divine to stand in the way of the union of the people of God. We do not care to discuss this question more particularly now, because we are satisfied that when all other grave difficulties shall have been overcome, this one will not long be allowed to stand.

V. We can never unite in non-essentials.

True; and it would not be worth much if we did. That is just the line we draw. In essentials — in that which is plainly taught and ordained as the will of God, we must be one; in non-essentials — in all that Christ has not taught and enjoined — we must be left free, guided only by that law of love which will ever lead us to seek the things that make for peace, and things wherewith one may edify another.

James Harvey Garrison

VICTOR HUGO in his William Shakespeare tells us that in the realm of high art there is no greatest poet. Homer, Virgil, Dante, Shakespeare are each supreme. Dante is different but just as great as Homer. So, Isaac Errett and J. H. Garrison, as editors of the *Christian Standard* and *The Christian Evangelist,* the one now wearing a crown of glory and the other still fighting valiantly the good fight of faith, have each been of first importance to the Restoration of Primitive Christianity — its doctrine, its ordinances, and its fruits. Mr. Errett was, and Mr. Garrison is the greatest protagonist of Christian liberty under the supreme authority of the Lord Jesus Christ in the line of noble men who have plead for Christian Union upon the New Testament basis. Both of them labored unceasingly with pen and voice for Christian Missions, and Mr. Garrison has been the especial champion of a larger recognition among the Disciples of Christ of the power and personality of the Holy Spirit in the development of Christian char-

335

acter and the progress of Christian Missions. He is a man of like passions with the rest of us who have our limitations, and being still one of us, we cannot fully appreciate all he has been to the Restoration of the Christianity of Christ as the method of restoring the unity of the body of Christ.

However, we need not wait until Mr. Garrison joins Barton W. Stone, Thomas Campbell, Alexander Campbell and Isaac Errett on the other shore to recognize the fact that if the responsibility of leadership in the balance of loyalty to the Word of God and liberty in the Son of God fell upon Mr. Errett when Mr. Campbell died, in 1866, the same responsibility fell upon Mr. Garrison, when Mr. Errett died, in 1888. The present generation of growing and aggressive Disciples of Christ owe more to Mr. Garrison than to any other living man for the liberty we enjoy in Christ Jesus. The champion of Christian missions, Christian liberty and Christian progress, he has ever recognized the supreme authority of our divine Lord and the New Testament alone as our guide in matters of doctrine and discipline.

James Harvey Garrison was born in Mis-

souri on the second day of February in
1842. At the age of fifteen he made a public
profession of religion and united with the Baptist church. After studying under C. P. Hall,
a Yankee school-teacher, young Garrison
taught a district school himself at the age of
sixteen. At the beginning of the Civil War
he was attending a high school at Ozark, his
birthplace. He identified himself with a company of Home Guards at Springfield, Missouri,
and after the battle of Wilson's Creek he en-
listed in the Twenty-fourth Missouri Infantry
Volunteers, and was severely wounded at the
battle of Pea Ridge, in March, 1862. Upon his
recovery he raised a company of cavalry volunteers and continued his services until the close
of the war, participating in several battles, acting as Assistant Inspector General and receiving the rank of Major for meritorious service.

When mustered out of the army in 1865, he
entered Abingdon College in Illinois and graduated in 1868 as Bachelor of Arts. The week
following his graduation he married Miss Ju-
dith E. Garrett, of Camp Point, Illinois, who
graduated in the same class with him, and has
been to him all that a faithful and affectionate

wife could be to her husband. In 1868 Mr.
Garrison and J. C. Reynolds jointly published
and edited the *Gospel Echo,* which was the fore-
runner of the *Christian Evangelist,* which, with
the *Christian Standard,* under the leadership
of Isaac Errett, became the two mighty advocates for Christian Missions, Christian Liberty
and Christian Progress. J. H. Garrison's influence in his preaching and writing has been
positive and spiritual rather than polemical
and controversial. He is the author of several
books; the most widely read, however, is the
one which is the truest expression of his own
personality, " Alone with God." As his biog-
rapher in the " Churches of Christ " has aptly
said: " All of his work, either as editor or
author, is in the very highest and best sense
purely Christian and always reflects the spirit
and teaching of the Word of God." Indeed, he
is the best representative of open-minded conservatism in Scriptural teaching and aggres-
siveness in the practical work of Christian
Evangelism, in the religious body of which
since the death of Isaac Errett, he has been the
acknowledged leader. Pleading for a larger
place for the Holy Spirit's power in the life of
the Christian, warning his brethren against

narrowness and the spirit of sectism, welcoming new light on old faiths, firm and free, J. H. Garrison is the leading living representative of the Disciples of Christ. His statement, the World's Need of Our Plea, is a fitting doc-. ument with which to close this volume of Historical Documents, which give the literary succession of the principles of the Restoration Movement of the Nineteenth Century.

JAMES HARVEY GARRISON.

The World's Need of Our Plea

BY J. H. GARRISON

The true standard by which men and movements, religions and reformations, must be measured, in their final test, is their capacity to minister to human need. Other worlds, for aught we know, may have other tests of merit, but in this disordered world of ours, where want and woe and sin and suffering abound, none other would seem to be adequate. Christ's mission to this earth, measured by any other rule than its fitness to supply human needs, must be considered a failure. If his incarnation, and death were not necessitated by man's wretched condition it would be impossible to find a justifying cause for these supreme facts of human history.

The infinite behoof that underlay the amazing condescension and the tragic death of the world's Redeemer, was man's helpless and hopeless condition. The transcendent value of Christianity consists in its ability to meet and satisfy the deepest wants of human nature. Eighteen centuries of Christian history attest its power to rehabilitate character, society, the family, the government and civilization. It follows, therefore, that the supreme need of this world is Jesus Christ, with all the plenitude of his truth and grace as revealed in the Gospel; and that religious movements or reformations are needful to the world in exact proportion to their ability to bring men to the knowledge and acceptance of Jesus Christ, and help them to be partakers of his nature and life. That all the successive reformations which have marked the history of the church, have contributed something to this end, and to that extent have served the needs of humanity, can not be denied.

It is our present purpose, however, to speak of the youngest of these great historical movements which have affected the life and thought of the world. In harmony with the principle just stated, if this movement of ours has any just claim on the sanction and sympathy, the acceptance and loyal support of the friends of God and humanity, it is because it comes bringing in its hands bread for the world's hunger, medicine for its wounds, and a corrective for its errors. It is my aim in this article to point out the correspondence between the world's needs and that which we have to offer. If it shall be seen that there is an intelligent and vital relation between this world's needs and that which we have to supply, then let no man ask, "By what authority doest thou these things?" for just as there is no higher authority for the use of any remedy than that it supplies what the diseased system needs, and restores it to its normal state, so there is no higher authentication of any religious reformation than that, to the extent its principles prevail, it neutralizes the morbid condition of religious society, restores Christianity to its normal condition, and removes out of the way those obstacles which tend to keep honest men away from Christ and the church; in a word, that it is adapted to the peculiar needs of the age which it seeks to serve.

As a patient requires different modes of treatment in the different stages of his disease, so this diseased world, at different periods in its history, has demanded various reformations. Peter speaks of those to whom he writes as being "established in the present truth," by which he probably meant the truth that needed special emphasis in his time. So every age has its "present truth," which needs pronounced advocacy, and that truth is the uncompromising antagonist of the " present " *error.* The Biblical affirmations of truth were determined, largely, by the then existing forms of error, so much so that some one has said that error is the matrix in which truth has been molded, in different ages. Hence it follows that truth adapted to one time, and to one condition of the church and of the world, does not meet the demands of a different time and a different state of the church. In this fact we may find room for the generous recognition of the service rendered to the world by previous reformations, without abating aught of zeal for our own plea, which emphasizes, as I believe, " the present truth "— that is, the truth which our own century and the present needs of the world require. If it be said that, according to this view, our own movement will in time be outgrown, and another reformation be demanded, my reply is that such will certainly be the result, if the plea we make shall become stereotyped, like those of previous reformations, instead of being a living, growing, adjustable movement, capable of adapting itself to the changing needs of the world, and the ever-shifting forms of error. We have wisely refused to stereotype by formulating a written creed, having profited by the experience of others, and if we shall succeed in avoiding the more subtle danger of stereotyping by the unwritten law of usage, or tradition, preferring life to crystallization, there is no reason why our plea, in its fundamental principles, should ever become obsolete. But of this, more later on.

A reformation implies a *de*formation, and must find its justifying cause in the condition of the religious world at the time it was inaugurated. No one can form a proper estimate of the strength and value of the Lutheran Reformation who does not understand the gross abuses and corruptions of the Romish Church at that time. These made a reformation an absolute necessity. There was nothing for honest and enlightened souls to do but to protest against the monstrous usurpations of authority and the unblushing violations of God's law by the Romish hierarchy. Not even the lion-hearted Luther and his able coadjutors could have so shaken Europe without this huge mountain of error and abuse to serve as the fulcrum for the lever of truth. The world needed Luther, and he came. It needed his reformation, and it succeeded. It was the *needs* of the age that gave occasion and vitality to the reformation of the sixteenth century.

This is true, also, of other reformations which succeeded and supplemented, to some extent, that of Luther. They were grounded in the abuses of their times, and demanded by those whose minds were enlightened with Biblical truth. If this be not true of the reformation which we plead, then it is an exception to all others, and is a phenomenon without an intelligible explanation or an adequate cause. But the careful student of church history will find in the condition of the church, in this country, at the beginning of the present century, many things that called loudly for religious reformation. At that time theology had largely run into metaphysics; or, perhaps it is more accurate to say that it had not yet recovered from the metaphysical hair-splitting of the preceding century. Christians owning the same Lord were separated from each other by an impassable chasm, because of differences of opinion on matters transcending human knowledge, and sustaining no vital relation to Christian life or character. Matters of opinion were confused with matters of faith, and often the former had far more to do in determining one's orthodoxy than the latter. As might be expected under such circumstances, party spirit ran high, and the spirit of true piety and brotherly love ran correspondingly low. As for that charity without which all our vaunted faith and knowledge are as nothing in the sight of God, it was sacrificed, often, on the altar of party. Christianity seems to have been regarded as a system of theological subtleties and abstractions to be defined and its definitions defended, rather than as consisting of personal loyalty to Christ and love to one another. The church was conceived of as made up of denominational " branches," which might have no fellowship with one another, because of doctrinal differences, rather than as the body of Christ, all of whose members should co-operate in carrying out the will of the Head. Christians fenced themselves apart, and Christ was crucified afresh in the dismemberment of his mystical body. Tradition, as in the time of our Savior, had made void some of the commandments of God, and had obscured the once plain way of salvation. The religious experiences of those times consisted, often, of dreams, visions, ecstasies of feeling, personal bouts with the devil, audible declarations of pardon from the Savior's lips, and other marvelous phenomena. Others less imaginative, failing to receive these wonderful signs, doubted the genuineness of their conversion, and were plunged into the depths of despair. It was no uncommon thing to find people who had been seeking Christ in this way many long years without being able to find Him, and there seemed to be none to point these confused souls to Christ, as the apostles directed inquiring sinners in the same condition. There was prevalent among the churches a kind of teaching, sometimes known as Calvinism, and often manifesting itself under other names among those claiming to be Arminians, which virtually robbed man of all responsibility, and made his salvation depend on conditions wholly external to himself, over which he had no control. It was not orthodoxy then, to teach that Christ's death brought salvation within the reach of all men, and that all could and should become Christians. Rather, it was taught that men had no power to accept Christ, until supernaturally called and quickened, not by the Gospel, which was a " dead letter," but directly by the spirit of God, and such a call, it was frequently taught, was reserved for the elect. The tendency of teaching was to cloud many sensitive souls with gloom and despair, and to drive others into scoffing skepticism.

This picture, so far from being overdrawn, might be painted in much darker colors without going beyond the truth of history. An age in which the Bible is practically displaced by creeds, and in which the disintegrating power of opinionism has destroyed the unity of the body, an age which gives more credence to feelings and impressions than to the plainest declarations of God's word, and subordinates the love of truth to the love of party, is one that *must* breed reformers, or witness the decadence of faith and the rejection of the church by the most thoughtful minds. In such an age was this Reformation born, and its birth-throes marked a new epoch in the history of the church, and opened a new and marvelous chapter in modern evangelism. It was a necessity. The bondage to creeds had become intolerable. Here and there, throughout all Christendom, and particularly in the United States, there were true and loyal hearts, turning away from religious bondage and superstition, for something better. The world was ripe for a movement which would furnish an antidote for the ills of a disordered Christendom. At such a time God always raises up a man or men of "light and leading," whose words focus the desires and aims of others, and whose towering personality becomes, for the time, a rallying-center for the forces of reform. Such men were not wanting in the beginning of this Reformation. But let us lose sight, for the time, of personal agencies, and seek to find in the *principles* advocated an antidote for the diseased condition of the religious world.

I. First of all, there was needed a remedy for the divisions in the church that Christ's prayer for the oneness of his disciples might be fulfilled. While this need was derided a half century ago, it has ceased to be derided now by intelligent people. The only question is as to the feasibility of the remedy proposed. This remedy was:

1. The abandonment of the use of uninspired creeds and confessions of faith, as bases of fellowship or as bonds of communion, and the restoration of the original, divinely inspired confession of faith, made by Simon Peter, upon which Christ said he would build his Church, to the place which it occupied in the Apostolic Church.

2. The disuse of party names unknown to the Scriptures, for scriptural, undenominational names, that Christ might have the pre-eminence in all things.

3. As to the divine law governing the life of the believer, the rule suggested was, " Where the Scriptures speak we speak, and where the Scriptures are silent we are silent." This would lead to the obedience of every plain commandment of Christ, and guarantee liberty in those things in respect to which the Scriptures are silent.

4. Hence, Christian character and conduct, and not opinions, were to be the test of fellowship among brethren who held to the " one Lord, one faith, and one baptism."

This simple basis of unity is commending itself more and more to thoughtful minds in all religious bodies. The exemplification of the practical character of this basis in the life and history of one of the leading Protestant bodies of this country has done much to remove the objection once made against it, that while it was a beautiful theory it was impracticable.

Never was the religious world so much in earnest on the subject of Christian unity as it is to-day, and never was there greater need for the vigorous presentation of the New Testament basis of union. If the religious movement inaugurated by Thomas and Alexander Campbell had done nothing more than to present this remedy for a divided church, it would amply have vindicated its right to an existence among the religious forces of Christendom. But it has accomplished more than this.

II. Next in importance to the plea for union made by the Campbells and their coadjutors, we reckon their great contribution to Biblical knowledge in the new and more rational method of treating the Holy Scriptures. From the state of things previously described it is obvious that the most superstitious ideas prevailed as to methods of interpretation. The King James' Version was regarded by many as too sacred to admit of revision! A profound mystical meaning was given to the most commonplace statements of the Bible, and there was little or no regard to the dispensation, time, or character of the writers. In opposition to all this Alexander Campbell taught that the Bible, while an inspired volume, must be interpreted according to the same common-sense rules which we apply to other literature; that we must put the particular book we are studying in its proper historic relations and setting, asking ourselves who the writer was, when he wrote, to whom he wrote, for what purpose, and under what conditions. All this, of course, was higher criticism, though he did not call it by that name. He also applied the inductive method of reasoning, which Bacon emphasized if he did not originate, to scriptural study, and urged the supreme importance of gathering all the inspired statements on any subject, and allowing them, in their free and unconstrained meaning, to form our view or theory on that subject instead of taking our theories to the Bible to find confirmation for them. Out of this free and independent method of Biblical study, there resulted a more scriptural, reasonable and consistent view of the whole subject of conversion,— involving the nature and office of faith, its relation to the Gospel and to obedience, the work of the Spirit, his mode of operation, the nature of repentance, the place of baptism and its relation to forgiveness of sins,— which, next to the plea for union, we regard as the most important contribution which the current Reformation has made to the religious thought of the age.

When it is remembered how men have

lived and died out of the church, and how many have been made skeptics through the irrational and unscriptural views and practices which have prevailed on the subject of conversion, it will be seen how great was the world's need of a Reformation which should brush away these false conceptions and present this great theme in a way to commend itself to the judgment and the conscience of men.

These two great cardinal features of the Reformation we plead — the plea for union on the original, apostolic basis, and the re-proclamation of the Gospel in its original simplicity and directness, stripped of the accumulated traditions and superstitions of past ages, will account in a large measure for the phenomenal success which has attended its advocacy. The world *needed* an antidote for these two great errors,— divisions among Christians and the obscuration of the once plain way of salvation — and because the Reformation presented a practicable remedy, it has succeeded beyond the most sanguine expectation of its originators. But there are many other features, which, though subordinate to the foregoing, help to give completeness and symmetry to a great historic movement.

WHAT HAS BEEN ACCOMPLISHED.

Elsewhere the writer has summarized the results of our reformatory work as follows:

1. In the strong emphasis it has laid on the evils of a divided church, and its victorious plea for Christian unity.

2. In pointing out those fundamental and catholic truths which constitute the scriptural basis of unity.

3. In the repudiation of the religious authority of all human creeds, or their use as bases of communion and fellowship.

4. In exalting the Word of God as the only authoritative and all-sufficient guide in religious faith and practice.

5. In the restoration of the New Testament confession of faith — the confession of Jesus as the Christ, the Son of the living God — as the foundation of the church and the only confession of faith precedent to baptism and church membership.

6. In demonstrating the practicability of preserving essential soundness in the faith and unity in religious teaching and practice, without the aid of a written authoritative rule of faith, other than the Holy Scriptures.

7. In its efforts to free the human mind and conscience from the fetters forged by past generations, thereby making possible what God evidently intends, perpetual progress in the knowledge of our Lord Jesus Christ and of his wonderful revelation.

8. In its return to, and practical use of, the apostolic methods of evangelization, namely, the simple presentation of Christ as the Savior of the world, and the urgent plea that those who sincerely propose to take Him as Lord and Savior should confess Him at once and enter upon the Christian life through the initiatory and confessional act of baptism.

9. In its removal of a vast amount of superstition and traditional usage which had accumulated about the subject of conversion, and presenting it in the clear light of the Gospel, which has been found to be in harmony with reason and with the laws of man's mental and moral constitution. This process has accentuated human responsibility without in the least discounting the divine power which operates, not in disregard of, but through our human faculties.

10. In teaching and disseminating a clear, rational and scriptural view of faith — its na-

ture, its object, its relation to divine testimony, and to salvation; that it is spiritual vision, leading to trust, has the personal Christ for its object, and not a dogma, comes by hearing the word of God, being based on divine testimony, and finds its end in salvation, because it leads the soul to commit itself to Christ in active, loving obedience. Thus discriminating between faith and opinion, it lifts the personal, historic Christ far above all human creeds and dogmas.

11. In discarding the unscriptural and antiscriptural phraseology with which the theological schoolmen of the past have obscured the greatest truths of revelation, and insisting on a return to the pure speech of the Bible, " calling Bible things by Bible names." Much of the controversy and many of the divisions of the past have grown out of these unbiblical phrases and definitions.

12. In stimulating the study of the Bible and promoting a clearer understanding of the relation of the different parts of the Bible to each other, and the nature of, and distinction between, the different dispensations of the divine government. Especially has the emphasis laid on the *inductive* method of studying the

Bible in order to ascertain the truth, been productive of incalculable good. It is receiving, now, recognition and indorsement by the ripest Biblical scholarship of the age.

13. In its restoration of the simple worship of the New Testament, with the weekly observance of the Lord's Supper as its central and controlling feature.

14. In uncovering and bringing to light once more that almost forgotten doctrine of the New Testament — the common priesthood of all Christians and the absolute equality of all believers in rights, privileges and spiritual prerogatives. "One is your Master and all ye are brethren."

15. In making prominent the *practical* and *ethical* side of Christianity, as against the emotional and theoretical side; in emphasizing ortho*praxy,* or right doing, as of greater value than ortho*doxy,* or right thinking; in discounting a faith that is purely sentimental, and insisting on a living faith that attests its vitality in good works. This conception of Christianity harmonizes well with the modern tendency, so full of promise, to apply the principles of the Gospel to the social evils of our times, as the only adequate remedy for a disordered so-

ciety, as they are for a disordered individual life.

A PROGRESSIVE REFORMATION.

III. One of the things which this world needs in order to its continuous approximation to that ideal state when the will of God shall be done on earth as it is in heaven, is a progressive reformation, which, by virtue of its underlying principles, will be held in loyalty to Christ, while it is capable of adjusting itself to the new phases of thought and of life as they arise, and of accepting all duly accredited truth, however new it may be. The creed of such a reformation must be nothing more or less than the essential truth of Christianity — the Messiahship and divinity of Jesus of Nazareth. The rule of its life and growth must be the will of Christ — its only Leader. Hence *restoration* must of necessity be the first step in such a reformation. That is, in order to such a continuous and orderly progress in truth as the religious world needs, there must be first a return to the simple, original constitution of the church, which was designed by its Author for infinite progress in the knowledge of the truth.

There have been many reformations in the history of the church which did not prove to be progressive reformations, because they were not based on the original creed of the church, which provides for expansion while demanding strictest loyalty to Christ. It is evident to every one who has given the subject careful and unbiased thought, that the modern elaborate creed or confession of faith is both an obstacle to progress and a frequent cause of division. The reformations alluded to crystallized their conclusions in fixed formulus, which were made tests of denominational fellowship and loyalty. Henceforth one must confine his theological thinking within these prescribed limits, under pain of trial for heresy, or of what is scarcely less to be dreaded, the *odium theologicum.* Hence it came to pass, as the good old Puritan pastor, John Robinson, said, that the followers of Luther and Calvin got no farther than their leaders, but stopped where they stopped. The reason for this stoppage, in the Lutheran Reformation, for instance, was the formulating of the theological opinions of that period into an authoritative creed, and making it a *ne plus ultra,* beyond which no adventurous keel was to push its way into unknown seas.

The Reformation inaugurated by the Campbells, in the first decade of the present century, was based, as its advocates claim, on a new *principle* of reformation. The Campbells saw the mistake of Protestantism in formulating its creed, and thus limiting its growth, and they proceeded on the principle that Jesus Christ had given his church the only creed it needed and that the only thing necessary to heal the divisions in the church and to promote its continuous growth in the knowledge and practice of the truth, was to restore the divine creed, and be loyal to all that it means and involves. In pursuance of this principle many important truths have been re-discovered and applied in the life and the work of the church, and many conclusions have been reached which have made faith easier, Christianity more reasonable, God more lovable, and human responsibility greater. These additions to religious knowledge have not been regarded in the nature of a new creed to be adopted and urged upon others as a test of fellowship, but as a contribution to the religious life and progress of the church, which exalts Christ, magnifies God's word and gives a wider and clearer view of the whole Christian economy.

Has the world's need for a progressive reformation been met in the plea which we make? It remains to be seen whether this movement holds within itself the indestructible elements of freedom and progress. Three or four scores of years is too short a time, perhaps, for fully testing its capacity to resist all the temptations which usually beset a religious reformation, and tend to divert it from its original aim, but so far it has shown sufficient vitality and loyalty to its basic principle to overcome whatever tendency there has been to crystallize into a sect and make further progress heresy. When men have broken with Christ and have proved disloyal to the divine creed, they have soon found that they had no place with us. But within the lines of this comprehensive though simple creed, there is abundant room for progress along all the lines of Christian thought. If this progress, which is fully provided for in the creed which we have accepted, is not made, if we fail to deal with the living questions of our day in the free and fearless manner which our Christian liberty warrants, or if we deal with them in a manner which takes no account of Christ's kingship, we shall in either case forfeit the vantage-ground which

our fathers gave us, and prove ourselves unworthy of a sacred trust. We shall then cease
to be a *current* Reformation. Then the Lord
will raise up others to voice his truth and plead
his cause; for whoever may fail, God's truth
will not fail, but will triumph over superstition, error, and every false way.

"Prove all things; hold fast that which is
good," is a motto which embodies both the bold
spirit of investigation and a wise conservatism.
These are not contrary one to the other. They
are the essential elements of a safe progress.
On the one hand the motto forbids that nervous
anxiety and excitement which become manifest
in harsh epithets, whenever a new view is presented or a position is taken differing from
that usually held. On the other, it cautions
against an undue readiness to accept a new
view because it is new, and to part with the
old because it is old. It may be "good" even
if it is old. It requires a fair and candid examination of all theories and positions before
accepting or rejecting them. Alas! how few
of us have the faith, the patience, the love of
truth and the forbearance to treat with proper
respect the man who dares to differ from us!
Than this there is scarcely any greater obstacle

to the ascertainment of truth. Let us hear with patience and with brotherly respect the honest convictions of every one who believes he has a new truth, or a new view of an old truth, to communicate to us.

This is not to be lenient to error, it is to be loyal to truth. Have we the catholicity of spirit, the love of truth, and the moral heroism and independence, to face the new and living questions of our day, in the same untrammeled way our reformatory fathers faced the questions of their day? On our ability to bear this supreme test, depends the question as to whether ours shall be a living and progressive Reformation, or a mere crystallization of past achievements.

Space forbids us to give much detailed statistical information showing the growth of the movement and what it is doing for the world's conversion, but the following brief statement will be of interest to the general reader:

The latest report of our statistical secretary gives us 1,220,841 members, 10,983 churches, and 6,507 ministers. It also shows that the churches gave for self-support last year, $6,-115,000; for general benovelence, $339,000; for foreign missions through our various agencies, $285,000; for home missions, state, district and national, $402,956; total amount for missions, home and foreign, $687,956. For all purposes $7,140,065.

This is a very creditable showing, when the time we have been engaged in such work and the circumstances surrounding us are considered. It is at least prophetic of great future possibilities.